Sewing

Packs, Pouches, Seats & Sacks

Sewing

Packs, Pouches, Seats & Sacks

30 **Practical Projects**

Betty Oppenheimer

**with Step-by-Step
Illustrations by the Author**

**STOREY
BOOKS**
Schoolhouse Road
Pownal, Vermont 05261

The mission of Storey Communications
is to serve our customers by publishing practical information
that encourages personal independence in harmony with the environment.

Edited by Deborah L. Balmuth
Copyediting by Alicia Jones
Cover design by Rob Johnson, Johnson Design
Cover photograph by Kevin Kennefick
Text design by Cindy McFarland
Text production by Susan Bernier and Deborah Dailey
Finished project illustrations by Brigita Fuhrmann

The information in this book is true and complete to the best of our knowledge. All recommendations are made without guarantee on the part of the author or Storey Books. The author and publisher disclaim any liability in connection with the use of this information. For additional information please contact Storey Books, Schoolhouse Road, Pownal, Vermont 05261.

Storey Books are available for special premium and promotional uses and for customized editions. For further information, please call the Custom Publishing Department at 800-793-9396.

Printed in the United States by Bawden Printing
10 9 8 7 6 5 4 3 2 1

Library of Congress Cataloging-in-Publication Data

Oppenheimer, Betty, 1957–
        Sewing packs, pouches, seats, and sacks : practical projects / Betty Oppenheimer ;
    step-by-step illustrations by the author.
            p.   cm.
        "A Storey Book"
        ISBN 1-58017-049-8 (pbk. : alk. paper)
        1. Sewing. 2. Bags. 3. Household linens.   I. Title.
    TT715.067 1998
    646.2—dc21   98-13402
                                                                                   CIP

To those who taught me the needle arts, even when "women's work" was unpopular, and to those who taught me math and science, even though they were considered "men's work," I thank you for sharing your knowledge with me. The practical arts are ageless and without gender bias. Let us never allow social mores to cause us to forget how to make things by hand.

Contents

List of Projects by Degree of Difficulty

Level 1. Simple Sewing: Tarp • Shower Curtain • Vegetable Keeper • Jelly Bag Laundry Bag • Stuff Sack • Padded Handle Cover

Level 2. Some Skill Required: Harvest/Log Tote • Bandana Bundle • Apron Seed Packet Roll • Rigid Paintbrush Portfolio • Tool Roll • Grocery Bag Hanging Shoe Rack • Padded Shoulder Strap

Level 3. Fairly Challenging Construction: Elastic Towel Wrap • Passport Pouch Garment Bag • Bucket Caddy • Traveling Jewelry Roll • Hinged Stadium Seat Insulated Lunch Bag

Level 4. Complex Techniques and Construction: Sun Visor Organizer Water Bottle Shoulder Bag • Carpenter's Half-Apron • Mattress Pad or Cushion Cover

Preface

"**P**atience, Betty!** If you don't learn patience, you're going to have trouble getting on in the world." Oh, how I hated to hear Grandma Lillian say that! I raced through projects as fast as I could, thinking that speed meant prowess. Nothing ever happened fast enough or soon enough for me.

Sewing brings out the best and the worst in me. At best, I produce beautiful, functional pieces with my own hands and experience a personal calm brought on by the meditative nature of the work itself. At worst, I get impatient, edgy, and produce nothing but shredded fabric destined for the rag bin. There is a philosophical aspect to sewing and other needlework, which is similar, perhaps, to what I've heard about fishing: to do it well requires patience and diligence. For me, these traits have improved with time.

I think of Grandma often as I sew. In my youth, I learned many techniques, studied fabrics and sewing, and made hundreds of garments, stuffed animals, wall hangings, and shoulder bags. But even now, I do not consider myself an accomplished seamstress or pattern maker. My success is directly related to the degree of patience I can muster during the undertaking of a project. The slower and more diligently I work, the better my results. Grandma was right — in terms of sewing skills, and life skills, too.

I've heard many people say that they gave up sewing because nothing ever came out right. As a freshman in college, I made a mountain parka and a down vest, and for the next five years, every time I zipped them up or down, I was reminded of how quickly and how poorly I had attached the zippers. Sewing produces permanent results. I could have, and should have, taken the zippers

out and resewn them properly, but impatience got the better of me. The garments — intended to be practical, functional items — became symbols of my impatience.

Sewing is an art and a science that can contribute to our material and our spiritual growth. It speaks to the idea of basic human survival on the practical side, and of community and personal growth on the philosophical side. I enjoy and have honed my skills in the practical side of sewing: designing and making useful things. But through the years, I have become more focused on the quality of my work and the serenity and satisfaction that can be found in the actual process. When I find myself becoming impatient, I stop sewing and do something that requires less focus. I am deliberate in my attempt to find and enhance the spiritual side of sewing, the satisfaction of a job well done, and the quiet, introspective time spent creating beautiful things and building my levels of patience and diligence.

This is a practical book, written to impart an understanding of the science of designing and customizing useful items. It does not require spiritual endeavor, or expert-level pattern-making and sewing techniques. What is necessary is a few basic materials and a desire to spend some time learning a new skill. If you choose, use this book on a purely practical level. Or, you can join me in the philosophical approach to sewing, the approach that ultimately improved my skills more than book learning. Take your time, be conscious of your mood, feel the textures of the fabrics, listen to your heart, and truly enjoy the art of sewing. If you are like me, you'll find that by following these suggestions, the end results, both material and spiritual, will be quite satisfying.

Introduction to Practical Sewing

The projects in this book are practical. They are items that I have had reason to make over the years, as gifts or for my own use. Often, patterns for practical items are hard to find, so I have experimented, examined mass-produced versions of similar items, and learned to "sculpt" with fabric. The aim of this book is to teach you to do the same.

Chapter 1 discusses the basics: the equipment you'll need and the types of fabrics available. In chapter 2, sewing techniques and tools are addressed. I recommend that all readers, no matter your skill level, read or at least review these chapters before attempting a project. For your convenience, cross references to particular sewing techniques have been added to the projects, so that you can revisit the step-by-step technique instructions if necessary. Then the real fun begins — the projects themselves.

Chapters 3 through 7 present a variety of projects for all skill levels: from beginners to experienced sewers. They are very simple shapes and require much easier stitching techniques than those involved in making a tailored garment. Cutting layouts are provided for most projects, to help you use your fabric wisely. Shading on the layouts indicates the fabric face.

If you've never sewn before, you can learn and develop your skills while creating these projects. The projects are organized in order of complexity, beginning with simple, flat shapes, and progressing into various pockets, bags, and fasteners. Combining specific shapes with various sewing techniques allows for an infinite array of designs. All of these sewing projects can be done in an afternoon or a day, and then put to immediate use.

As you create the projects in this book, you will gain the experience needed to design your own practical projects. The experience of turning flat fabric into a functional three-dimensional item will spark your creativity, and with some practice, you will soon be able to design and construct many sewn items.

The book concludes with a chapter to get you thinking practically about the design process. It encourages you to ask questions — lots! — about the function of a particular piece, and to design first on paper and then on muslin before finally cutting it out on the desired fabric. Form follows function, but questions and technical design can inspire creative solutions and problem-solving that will make the completion and use of your unique design incredibly satisfying. There is a great feeling of self-sufficiency, capability, and creativity in building these skills.

Learn by Doing

To learn through practice means to be willing to experiment. This is where technical know-how and creativity meet — your ideas can be put into practice to the extent that you are willing to experiment. Go ahead and make mistakes, try again, and learn new techniques through trial and error.

> *Practice is the best of all instructors.*
> — PUBLICUS SYRUS, *MAXIM 439*

I hope that you enjoy learning the basic techniques and making the designs in this book. As you progress, you may find that once the techniques are learned, the most valuable skills are those of the imagination. Being able to visualize that which does not yet exist and a willingness to play with fabric shapes to invent what is in the mind's eye are the beginnings of true creative sewing.

Design Your Own Patterns

Throughout the book I have tried to explain how and why I designed particular aspects of each project as I did. These observations are offered to give you a perspective on my thought processes, from the beginning of an idea, to paper, and finally to fabric. I hope that these explanations are useful, and help you to begin to personalize the projects and the process to fit your own working style and sewing ideas. If you use this book as a springboard to greater sewing freedom and creativity, then I will have succeeded in my efforts at teaching practical sewing.

You can design your own patterns! Basic sewing skills, the patience to make and rework mistakes, and a willingness to tap into your own creativity are all it takes to become a practical pattern maker. Don't let the ease of buying patterns dissuade you from making your own. Rarely does a purchased pattern contain every design element you had in mind, so don't be afraid to modify them or any other pattern. The end product will be more your own, and the personal reward will be greater.

Remember, these projects are like blank slates waiting to be embellished. Surface design, like painting, stenciling, stamping, and printing, as well as needlework designs, such as beading and embroidery, can further personalize the finished product. Although I have not discussed embellishment at great length in these pages (see the Suggested Readings section for a list of books on the subject), let me be the first to wholeheartedly encourage you to decorate your work. Usefulness does not preclude beauty. In the words of William Morris, one of the greatest designers of the Arts and Crafts movement, "If you want a golden rule that will fit everybody, this is it: Have nothing in your houses that you do not know to be useful, or believe to be beautiful" (*The Beauty of Life*, 1880).

Selecting the Right Equipment and Fabric

one

To make your sewing experience most enjoyable and your finished projects as useful as possible, you need to have the right equipment on hand and know how to select the most appropriate fabric, one that will stand up to the functions it is expected to perform. In this chapter, you'll learn everything you need to know to acquire the right materials and get set up. I suggest reading through this chapter before you begin and then returning to it as you prepare to create specific projects, particularly to learn more about the types of fabric you will need for each.

Sewing Machine

A special machine is not necessary to create these projects, since they do not require any fancy stitches (although you can, of course, use them for embellishment, if you wish). Since only straight stitching is used, a good basic machine is all you need.

Machine Requirements

Your machine should have forward- and reverse-stitching capabilities. The sewing in these projects often requires going through many layers of upholstery-weight fabric, which can be hard work for your machine. Therefore, a heavy-duty machine is a plus: It gives you more flexibility, allowing you to sew light-, medium-, and heavy-weight fabrics. Most machines made prior to the 1960s are considered heavy duty by today's standards.

My local sewing sales and service man estimates that the cost of purchasing a good, basic used machine is between $150 and $300; new machines range from $150 to $5,000. If you have an older machine that you've inherited or haven't used in a while, it can be brought up to speed with a tune-up service, which costs about $50 (not including parts). If properly maintained, an older machine can sew as well as a new one. Many of the new, inexpensive machines on the market are light duty; pushing them to their limit can result in broken gears and lots of time at the sewing service center. So if you are planning to buy a sewing machine and don't want to spend a lot of money, consider a reconditioned used machine instead of a new one.

In terms of the machine's accessories, you will need both a standard presser foot (the metal piece that drops down to hold the fabric in place, and helps feed it through the needle area) and a zipper foot. The zipper foot allows you to stitch much closer to raised edge or thicker areas of fabric, and is used to attach zippers and make welting, as well as to do other applications.

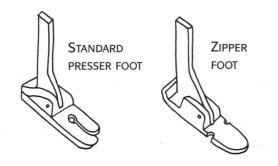

STANDARD PRESSER FOOT

ZIPPER FOOT

Tuning Up Your Machine

It is important to keep your machine properly tensioned and well oiled. If there's one thing I've learned over the years, it's the value of an annual sewing machine tune-up. If your machine hasn't been oiled and tuned for a while, have it done before you embark on these projects.

There are also several maintenance tasks you can perform at home to keep your machine functioning properly. First, be sure to store your machine in a dry place at room temperature; cold or moisture can cause the machine to malfunction. Second, guard against improper tension and excess lint, the two most common and troublesome machine problems.

WHAT YOU NEED TO KNOW ABOUT YOUR MACHINE

Before starting on a project in this book, be sure you know how to perform the following functions on your machine:

- Threading
- Winding and inserting a bobbin
- Adjusting stitch length and thread tensions
- Changing a needle
- Sewing forward and backward

If you don't have a manual for your machine, take it to a sewing service store and ask the personnel to show you how to perform these basic techniques (it might be a good idea to get a tune-up done at the same time). Most sewing repair people are glad to show you the right way to use your machine. They can label the various thread points so you won't forget how to thread the machine, and they might even be able to get you a manual for your particular model.

Adjusting stitch tensions. Proper thread tension is critical in any sewing project, because too little or too much will weaken your seams or cause your fabric to pucker. Be sure to learn how to adjust both the upper and lower tension controls. The upper tension control on your machine regulates the underside loops of stitching; the screw on the bobbin case regulates the top loops: If the stitch loops appear irregular on the underside, adjust the upper tension control; if the stitch loops appear irregular on the top surface, adjust the screw on the bobbin case.

Tension can also be thrown off by the use of poor-quality thread, which can be fuzzy and have inconsistent thickness. Be sure to buy new, mercerized, high-quality thread for use in your sewing machine; and if you have old wooden spools of thread, use them only for hand sewing.

Removing fiber lint and dirt. Lint that accumulates under the machine's needle plate (the metal plate that the needle passes through) causes the plate to rise slightly. This, in turn, throws off the mechanism that feeds your fabric into the machine. Sewing then becomes more difficult, as the motor and gears compensate for the poor fabric feeding. You can clean this area (and the rest of the bobbin case) yourself by frequently removing the needle plate and vacuuming out as much lint as you can. A lint brush with nylon bristles, or an old toothbrush works well, too.

Sewing Supplies

The sewing supplies and equipment you will need to undertake the projects in this book can be found at any sewing supply store. The following are some recommendations regarding specific supplies.

Needles and Pins

Purchase high-quality sewing machine needles to fit your brand of sewing machine. You will notice that there are different needle sizes for light-, medium-, and heavy-duty fabrics. The heavy-weight fabrics used in many of these projects will require size 14, 16, or 18 needles. Keep extras on hand — you may break a needle stitching through some of the heavier fabrics. Ideally, needles should be replaced after three hours of actual sewing time.

For hand stitching, embroidery needles are best, since they are heavy and sharp. A combination pack of needles will contain most of what you'll need. However, for stitching closed a welted (piped) seam, you may want to have a curved needle.

For pins, I like to use the ones with ball heads, because they are easy to find if dropped. When working with thick fabrics, pin length is an issue; extra-long pins are best for holding thick or layered fabrics together.

Thread

Your thread choice depends on the weight and fiber content of the fabric being stitched. Standard cotton-wrapped polyester thread is recommended for medium-weight projects, and is generally a size 40–60. You can use 100 percent cotton thread, if you prefer, but make sure it is mercerized to give it the strength it needs to run at high speeds through the sewing machine. For some of the heavier cotton projects, heavy-duty, quilting, or button and carpet thread is best, as they are stronger and abrasion resistant.

For heavy nylon projects and for padded items, I recommend using nylon upholstery thread. It holds up under the pressure of your body (when used to make mattresses or kneeling pads, for example) or under the added weight of clothing or tools (which you may put in sewn containers such as a duffel bag or a carpenter's apron). Heavier threads are also necessary when sewing leather or vinyl laminates, since the abrasion caused by the needle passing in and out of the fabric wears on the thread. It is also a good idea to use heavier thread when sewing gathers, to make sure that it doesn't break as you pull the stitches to gather the fabric.

Scissors and Other Cutting Tools

A pair of sharp scissors is a must. In fact, your fabric scissors (shears) should be used exclusively for fabric. I label mine "fabric only" with a piece of masking tape so that no one accidentally uses them on paper or cardboard, which will dull their edges. With fabrics that are heavy and slippery, the only way to cut a clean, sharp line is to use sharp scissors. Professional sharpening services are available at many fabric and sewing stores.

A newer tool on the market is the rotary cutting wheel, which is great for cutting straight lines and is much easier on the hands than scissors. Make sure you have a sharp blade. To cut curves, a variety of templates, including french curves, can be used as guides for the cutting blade. You'll also need a rubberized cutting mat to place under the fabric to protect your tabletops from the sharp cutting wheel. These accessories are all available at fabric and sewing

stores. Spring-loaded scissors with cushioned handles (which are similar in design to some garden pruners) are another relatively new tool that causes less strain on the hands than conventional scissors.

Measuring and Marking Tools

The project patterns in this book can be drawn directly onto your fabric (see chapter 2, page 20). To do so, you will need a straightedge ruler. I use a 36-inch T square for measuring out the long lines, and an 18-inch metal ruler for marking the more detailed points. A wide, transparent quilting rule with measured markings across the width and down the length is also handy for making incremental measurements.

I recommend always using chalk for marking the face (right side) of the fabric. Tailor's chalk, which comes in flat chunks or pencil form, works well for marking the pattern layout, although the lines drawn are often wide and may rub off as you work. To avoid problems, use the pencil form, sharpened to the finest point possible, and then handle the fabric carefully to avoid rubbing off the chalk lines.

For marking the back of the fabric or in the seam allowances, I often use a fine-line felt-tip marker or ballpoint pen. This gives a very accurate line, which will not show in the finished piece, as long as you mark only in the concealed areas of the fabric. Avoid using water-soluble inks; they can bleed through to the face of the fabric during laundering.

Iron

You will need a good basic steam iron with an adjustable temperature control. An ironing board is not essential — a table protected with a towel works just as well.

SELECTING NEEDLE AND THREAD SIZE, AND LENGTH OF STITCHES

Before starting a project, follow the recommendations in this chart to choose the most appropriate needle and thread sizes, and adjust the stitches per inch on your machine to get the best results for the fabric you are stitching.

FABRIC WEIGHT	NEEDLE SIZE	THREAD NUMBER	STITCHES PER IN.
Sheer	9–11	70	16–18
Light-weight	11	60	14–16
Medium	11–14	50	12–14
Heavy	14–16	40	10–12
Extra Heavy	16–18	*	6–10

*Button and carpet, or nylon upholstery

Selecting Fabrics

Practicality is an important feature to consider when selecting, the fabric and components used to make the projects in this book. A basic understanding of the materials you choose will improve your final product. If you've sewn at all, I'm sure you've had the experience of making a garment only to discover it did not meet your expectations, in terms of *durability* (how long it lasts), *washability* (how much it shrinks), *abrasion resistance* (how well it resists becoming fuzzy and pilled on its surface), *resiliency* (the ability to stretch out and spring back), *tear strength* (its tendency to resist ripping), or *fiber content, breathability,* and *hand* (level of wearing comfort). These and many other terms are common language in the textile industry, and are characteristics that can be controlled and predicted during the development and manufacture of any fabric. As a consumer, being knowledgeable about these factors can save you from choosing poor materials that, with time, render the items you have sewn useless.

The terms commonly used to describe various types of fabric often make reference to fiber content (cotton, wool, acrylic) and construction (weave or knit). There are also some age-old fabric names, such as calico, canvas, and lawn, that offer few clues as to what the fabric is actually made of. Even experienced sewers may not know as much as they'd like to about the performance characteristics of a fabric that goes by one of these "mystery" names. Fabric mills and manufacturers have specialized tests for assessing the performance characteristics of a given fabric. They evaluate fiber content, weight, thickness and hand, absorbency and breathability, durability, yarn size and thread count, and fabric construction and its impact on other significant qualities. You can use these same factors to analyze and define the makeup of a particular piece of fabric.

Fiber Content

Fabrics are made of various kinds of fibers, some natural, some synthetic. Each fiber has its own set of characteristics, including benefits and drawbacks (see chart, page 8). When fibers are combined to make fabric, these characteristics are present in the finished product. For many of the projects in this book, cotton and nylon are the most logical fabric choices: Cotton is generally used for items that you want to be soft or decorative, and nylon is for rugged outdoor use. There is no reason to limit yourself to cotton and nylon, however. Read the chart on page 8 for other possible options.

Weight

In the industry, fabrics are referred to by the number of ounces in a square yard (36 x 36") or in a linear yard (36" length x the width of the cloth). Weight per square yard is the most accurate and useful method for comparing fabrics. For example, most jeans are made of 14-ounce denim (i.e., there are 14 ounces in a square yard). From experience, we know that this is a heavy and durable weight of cloth that holds up well to wear. Based on this knowledge, you might use a 14-ounce canvas for many of the heavier-duty projects in this book. (See the chart on page 13 for common fabric names by weight and weave.)

Thickness and Hand

These are qualities you will need to assess to determine whether a particular fabric meets the expectations for the intended project. When assessing fabric thickness, you will need to take into account the total number of fabric layers in the completed project: Will your machine be able to stitch through this thickness? Will the resulting seam be too thick? When evaluating

COMMON FIBERS AND KEY ATTRIBUTES

	BENEFITS	DRAWBACKS
COTTON	Strong, durable	Wrinkles
	Stronger when wet	Mildews
	Dyes well	Weakened by sunlight
	Does not pill or slip	Shrinks
	Breathable, absorbent	
RAYON	Breathable, absorbent	Wrinkles
	Dyes well	Seams slip
	Does not pill	Shrinks
		(Dry clean)
LINEN	Breathable, absorbent	Wrinkles
	Strong	Wears, brittle
	Does not pill	Does not dye well
		Shrinks
		Mildews
SILK	Wrinkle resistant	Conducts static electricity
	Strong and fine	Yellows, fades
	Absorbent	Weakened by sunlight
	Resists mildew, moths	
	Dyes well	
WOOL	Wrinkle resistant	Weaker when wet
	Elastic, shapes easily	Susceptible to mildew, moths
	Abrasion resistant	Pills
	Breathable, absorbent	Conducts static electricity
	Warm	
ACETATE	Resists mildew, moths	Wrinkles
	Does not shrink	Conducts static electricity
	Stable*	Fades
	Good for linings	Weakened by sunlight
		Not very strong
ACRYLIC	Wrinkles	Conducts static electricity
	Light-weight	Not very absorbent
	Quick drying	Pills
NYLON	Wrinkle resistant	Not very absorbent
	Dries fast	Faded by sunlight
	Elastic	Melts
	Resists mildew, mold	Pills
POLYESTER	Wrinkle resistant	Conducts static electricity
	Resists mildew, mold	Seams slip
	Strong	Pills
	Does not shrink	

Low shrinkage and a tendency not to distort (i.e., to twist or shift off grain).

the hand, or feel, of a fabric, you should base your decision on personal preference and perception of how you would like the finished item to feel. Is the fabric soft? Sticky? Does it appear to have a surface finish on the face or on the back? How will this finish affect the usefulness of your project?

Absorbency and Breathability

These two characteristics are very important to consider when selecting a functional fabric. Fabrics with good absorbency and breathability make very comfortable outdoor clothing, since they wick moisture away from your body, where it can then evaporate. For outdoor gear, however, absorbency can be a real problem. On a humid day, for example, an absorbent gear bag can become damp, mildew, and get very heavy just from the weight of the moisture. Select fabrics that fit the function of the item: The difference between a water-absorbent fabric and a water-repellent one really matters when making something that might be used out in the rain.

Durability

The durability of a particular fabric is determined by fiber, yarn, weave, and finish. Some predictions regarding durability can be made about a particular fabric by pulling on it lengthwise, widthwise, and diagonally (on the bias), to test its stability and stretch, and by scratching the fabric's surface to see whether it mars easily or shows signs of wear. Try pulling out yarns in both directions to see if the fabric has a tendency to fray. Run your thumbnail across the yarns to see whether the weave slips along the seamlines in the warp or weft direction. Look for *floats* (long spans of yarn "floated" across the fabric surface before being woven back in; usually decorative), which can snag on hook and loop (Velcro) or fingernails. Fabrics with surface finishes are often more durable; however, some finishes abrade easily and may wash off. Therefore, take into account how often the item will be laundered before choosing a finished fabric.

Yarn Size and Thread Count

In the textile industry, fabric construction is assessed in terms of the size of the yarn used to make the fabric, and how many yarns per inch are woven into the fabric. *Yarn size* is based on the weight of the yarn. The number of yarns per inch in the resulting fabric is known as the *thread count*. A fabric composed of strands of densely woven yarn is quite different from one made from thick yarns woven more loosely, yet it is possible for both fabrics to have the same weight.

Other Significant Fabric Characteristics

There are several specialty fabrics that have been constructed or treated to add certain attributes. A basic understanding of the following water and fire treatments can come in handy.

Water resistance. Water resistance can be achieved by applying a finish, or may be a part of the fiber or fabric's makeup. Wool and many synthetic fibers have a natural ability to resist absorbing water. Water-resistant fabrics offer the least protection against water; for outdoor use a heavier finish is required.

TAKING A CLOSER LOOK: DETERMINING THREAD COUNT

You may be surprised to learn how easy it is to determine the thread count of a piece of fabric. All you need is a pick glass, which is a magnifier hinged onto a 1-inch square measuring device. (Pick glasses are available at sewing shops, optical centers, and by mail.) Place a corner or 1-inch square of fabric under the glass in a well-lit location and, using a needle or other small pointer, count the warp (lengthwise) and weft or filling (widthwise) threads. You may need to unravel the end and selvage of the fabric so you can see the ends of the yarns.

You can also analyze the weave of the fabric. Is it plain, twill, satin, or novelty? (See page 13). Pull out some warp and weft yarns to determine the composition of the fabric. Often you will find a variety of yarn sizes and twists, some plied and others single. (*Twist* is how tightly, and in what direction, fibers are spun together. *Plied yarns* are made of several individual single yarns [plies] twisted together to form a stronger yarn.)

The more you look at fabric this way, the better you will understand what makes one type soft and another stiff; one thin and another bulky. You'll also begin to understand the various construction techniques. For example, if you look at terrycloth under the pick glass, you can visualize the pile weaving process.

PICK GLASS OR LINEN COUNTER

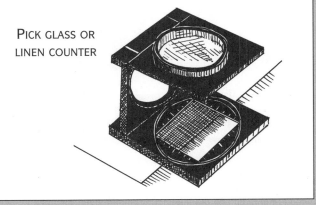

HOW IS FABRIC CONSTRUCTED?

Fabrics are commonly defined by the method of construction used: knit, nonwoven, or woven. You may have heard these terms and wondered exactly what they mean. This quick overview of fabric construction techniques will help you understand the strengths and weaknesses of various fabrics.

Knitted Fabrics

Weft-knit fabrics are constructed much like hand-knit sweaters, with rows of interlocking loops of yarn running along the width of the fabric. The vertical columns formed by the loops are called *wales;* the horizontal rows of loops are called *courses.* Knitted weft fabrics, such as jersey, rib knits, and interlock knits, tend to have a great deal of stretch. Warp-knit fabrics are made up of vertical columns of chain stitches that are joined by horizontal zigzags. Tricot is an example of a warp knit. Since they tend to be quite stretchy, knit fabrics are not desirable for many of the projects in this book, but you may find practical uses for using knit-backed vinyls or knitted velours.

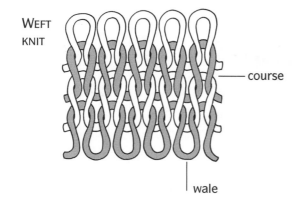

WEFT KNIT

course

wale

Nonwoven Fabrics

These fabrics are produced by the mechanical or chemical process of matting fibers together. One example of a nonwoven fabric is wool felt, formed when wool fibers bond naturally under the influence of moisture, heat, and agitation. Other nonwoven fabrics are formed artificially when heat and resins are used to adhere the fibers together. Fusible interfacing is a common example of a nonwoven fabric; it is treated with heat-activated resins that make it easy to adhere to other fabric with an iron. The performance of a nonwoven fabric depends on the intricacies of its construction — specifically, whether the fibers are random or aligned.

Woven Fabrics

Woven fabrics are the ones you are probably most familiar with. These are constructed on a loom, with the yarns woven at right angles to each other. The lengthwise yarns are called the *warp;* the widthwise yarns are called *weft* or *filling yarns.* Woven fabrics can be very plain or highly decorative, stable or flimsy, dense or transparent. There are four main types: plain weaves, twill weaves, satin weaves, and novelty weaves. Most of the fabrics recommended in this book are plain and twill weaves. You may, however, want to experiment with the other types.

Plain weaves. This pattern makes a very stable fabric, including such familar favorites as cheesecloth, muslin, chambray, flannel, and canvas.

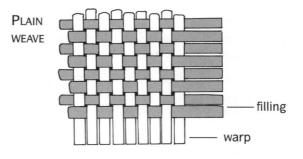

PLAIN WEAVE

filling

warp

Twill weaves. Twill weaves are very durable. Denim, gabardine, and serge are common examples. These fabrics are most easily identified by the diagonal, or stair, pattern formed by the weave pattern. Variations on the twill weave produce herringbone patterns, heavy ridges (wales), or diagonal ridges. If the wales and the valleys between them are the same size, the twill is even; if they differ in size, the twill is uneven.

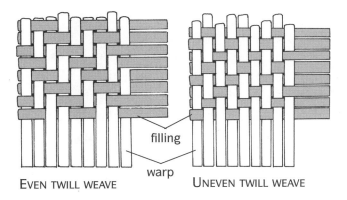

EVEN TWILL WEAVE   UNEVEN TWILL WEAVE

filling
warp

Satin and sateen weaves. This pattern is a variation on the twill weave and is sometimes called *skipped twill* or *reorganized twill*. These fabrics, which include damask, satin, and satin crepe, are commonly used for garments and home furnishings. Long "floats" of yarn run over the surface of the fabric to create a smooth, lustrous finish. Floats running along the warp (length) of the fabric produce a satin. Floats running across the filling (width) of the cloth produce a sateen. Since this fabric construction is not as durable as a regular twill, you might want to use a satin weave only as a decorative outer cover for some of the projects in this book.

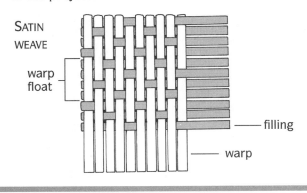

SATIN WEAVE

warp float

filling

warp

Novelty weaves. With the development of new textile equipment, variations on traditional weaves have emerged.

- **Pile weaves** are made by weaving an extra set of yarns into the surface of a plain woven or knitted base. Sometimes these extra yarns are left as loops to make fabrics such as terrycloth (all attached to a woven base); other times they are sheared, creating fabrics such as velvet, velour, and polar fleece (all attached to a knitted base).
- **Jacquard weaves,** with complex tapestry designs, are woven on computerized looms that are programmed to send the proper colors into the proper picks of the loom.
- **Leno weaves** are made by twisting the warp yarns between weft yarns, which prevents the weave from slipping and creates a thin, stable fabric. This technique is used to make everything from mosquito netting to lacy curtain fabrics.

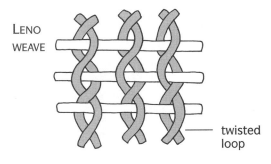

LENO WEAVE

twisted loop

- **Laminates** are produced by fusing together layers of various woven, knit, or nonwoven materials. Flannel may be laminated to denim to produce a lined garment; foam may be laminated to vinyl for car upholstery. Reflective metallic sheets can be laminated to insulating fiber to use in drapes. Technology continues to devise new uses for the lamination process. You may decide to use a laminate for some of the projects in this book.

Water repellence. This is a finish achieved by coating the surface of the fabric, using waxes, resins, or various combinations of chemicals. Since the pores of the fabric are not sealed during this process, the fabric still breathes (allows air to pass through), and thus tends to be comfortable to wear. Water-repellent fabrics are rated on a scale from spot resistant to shower-proof; they are not waterproof. Bear in mind that surface finishes do *not* waterproof seams — you will need to treat seams with a seam sealer.

Waterproofing. This finish seals the pores of the fabric with chemicals or coats the fabric entirely with a compound such as vinyl, thus preventing water penetration. Waterproof fabrics are not the best choice to use for clothes, but work well for many of the projects in this book.

Recent developments in fiber and fabric technology have yielded products such as Gore-Tex, which has breathable pores that are too small for water molecules to penetrate. Thus, it is a physically waterproof fabric that still allows the skin to breathe.

Fire resistance and fireproof. All natural fibers burn — that's a fact. The test for garment flammability (required by The Flammable Fabric Act of 1953) tests the rate of combustibility. Brushed or napped fabrics, such as flannels, chamois cloth, and fleece (sweatshirts), usually fail these tests. The brushed surface "flash burns," meaning that when a spark or ember catches a fiber end the whole surface of the garment is engulfed in flames within a split second. This tendency is reduced with washing; however, I make sure that I never wear a new flannel shirt or an inside-out sweatshirt near a campfire or any open flame. Synthetic fabrics can be even more dangerous, since instead of forming an ash, they melt into very hot, sticky globs that adhere to the skin. These fabrics can be treated with fire-retardant chemicals to slow the spread of flames.

Recommended Fabrics for Practical Sewing

Although I recommend using fabrics ranging from cotton cheesecloth to nylon pack cloth to make the practical projects in this book, please do not feel bound to using only the fabrics I recommend. There are so many choices these days that I could not begin to list them all. I hope that reading about how I select my favorites will help you understand what to consider when selecting fabric; you can then assemble your own list of favorites. Don't be afraid to unleash your creativity! My only warning is this: Fashion fabrics are often produced solely for their visual appeal, not for their performance. To make durable, functional items, you must choose fabrics that meet or exceed normal expectations for their intended use.

Cheesecloth (Gauze)

This is a loosely woven cotton fabric, made of single, twisted yarns. Cheesecloth is useful in the kitchen and makes an excellent strainer for paint, jellies, and gravies. It does not hold up well during complex sewing applications and is generally considered disposable.

Muslin

This plain-weave fabric, generally made of cotton or a blend of polyester and cotton, is often used for interior linings, unexposed layers of upholstery, and for test-sewing patterns. The name of this fabric changes as the thread count and weight increase: muslin (35–60 threads per inch), sheeting (80–140 threads per inch), or percale (up to 220 threads per inch). These fabrics are strong, smooth, easy to sew, and are often printed. They generally have balanced thread counts; that is, the warp and filling

SOME COMMON FABRIC NAMES BY WEIGHT AND WEAVE

WEIGHT	WEAVE			
	PLAIN	**TWILL**	**NOVELTY**	**NONWOVEN**
Light (0–4 oz. per sq. yd.)	Chiffon Challis Voile Organdy Batiste Lawn	Surah Foulard	Mosquito netting Lace	Feather-weight interfacing Saran
Medium (5–9 oz. per sq. yd.)	Calico Gingham Broadcloth Oxford Chambray Sheeting Poplin	Flannel Serge Gabardine Khaki cloth Covert cloth Denim	Damask Chenille Terrycloth Corduroy Velveteen Marquisette	Medium-weight interfacing Felt
Heavy (10 oz. and heavier)	Melton Burlap Repp Sailcloth Duck Buckram	Prunella Ticking Whip cord Drill	Velour Brocade Tapestry Upholstery	Heavy-weight interfacing Vinyl

counts are very similar, so the shrinkage is usually balanced.

Poplin

This is a tightly woven fabric made with many fine warp yarns and coarser filling yarns. It is a good, basic medium-weight fabric, often composed of cotton or a cotton/polyester blend, and is frequently used in uniforms due to its excellent durability. There are dozens of medium-weight plain-weave fabrics — too many to name here. Walking through your fabric store, feeling fabrics, and reading bolt labels will help you identify what you like. With practice, you will be able to identify fiber content with your fingertips.

Gabardine

The durable twill weave and medium weight (8 ounces) of this fabric make it a strong and versatile choice. It can be made of cotton, wool, or a blend that includes polyester or rayon. Wool gabardine is often used for suits. For the projects in this book, I recommend a cotton or cotton/polyester blend.

Heavier Twills

Names vary, but once you familiarize yourself with the feel of a gabardine (a medium-weight twill), you'll know a heavier twill when you feel one. I love using these heavy twills for bags, tool rolls, and in numerous other applications. They are durable, soft, easy to sew, and strong, but don't add excessive bulk. Denim is a type of heavy twill in which the warp yarns are white, and the filling yarns are dyed indigo blue (or, as we have seen in fashion jeans, green or red), resulting in the mottled effect. Denims, and other medium to heavy twills, range in weight from 7 to 14 ounces per square yard. Though many denims are prewashed these days, a natural aspect of indigo yarn dying is that the color bleeds onto the white threads during the first few washings, which produces the faded look we expect in our jeans. Be sure to wash all denim separately the first time or two.

SHEETS ARE EXTRAWIDE FABRIC!

Using bedsheets as fabric can be a relatively inexpensive way to get a lot of fabric. Older sheets can be used for linings and for testing patterns. Standard sheet sizes are:

Crib:	42 x 72"
Twin:	72 x 108"
Full:	81 x 108"
Queen:	90 x 120" (or 90 x 113")
King:	108 x 122"

Canvas

This tightly woven, plain-weave fabric is usually made of cotton fibers. Canvas can be 10 to 18 ounces, and is woven so tightly that it has some natural water-repellent properties. It is extremely durable and readily available. This fabric can be found in fabric and art stores, since it is also used in oil painting. Canvas is always available in unbleached, unfinished form, but it is also made with specific finishes (like waterproofing, for outdoor use) and patterns. Canvas is a great all-around choice for functional sewing.

Ripstop Nylon

This is a plain-weave fabric made of nylon fiber, with heavier yarns woven in at ¼-inch intervals that serve as "stop" threads, which prevent small tears from spreading. Nylon is used for tent rain flaps, stuff sacks, insulated vests, and outdoor gear. I have made shower curtains out of it, although it will absorb water if exposed to enough pressure and duration. A simpler version of this fabric is plain nylon taffeta, which does not have the ripstop feature. It is very inexpensive and functional: Use it for drawstring bags and other items in which light weight and some water resistance is desirable. Nylon taffeta can be slippery to sew, however, so it is best used with simple shapes only.

Pack Cloth

Most often a plain weave made of nylon, though it may sometimes contain polyester, this heavy cloth is among those used for making backpacks. It is technically a nylon canvas. Once only available through specialty outdoor suppliers, it can now be found in fabric stores. Use pack cloth for luggage, portfolios, outer coverings for sleeping bags, and any other application where weight, durability, and water repellence are important. More recently, texturized yarns have been used in constructing these cloths, making them softer and more visually interesting.

Vinyls and Various Laminated Fabrics

Although these fabrics are not very practical for clothing, the many waterproof options available these days have several valuable uses. Vinyl can be used as a waterproof outer shell or to line pockets in a cosmetic case, for example. Because of its poor breathability, vinyl is rarely used in clothing.

Vinyls are neither woven nor knitted, but rather extruded as a solid sheet, and are often laminated to other fabrics for aesthetic appeal or function. There are vinyls laminated to flannel; fabrics laminated to foam for thin, ready-made insulation; and all sorts of other combinations. I always keep small pieces of this fabric on hand, so I'm ready if I need it for something.

Fabric choice should be based on the intended use of the item being made. Leather, corduroy, upholstery fabrics (from velvets and tapestries to heavy-coated outdoor furniture fabrics), industrial fabrics, or layers of different fabrics work well for reversible or lined projects. Nylon mosquito netting is great to use for some outer pockets on specific items. A tool roll for an auto mechanic warrants heavy canvas or twill, while a tool roll made to hold makeup brushes could be made of beautiful brocade on the outside, with a flannel lining. Many of the projects in this book use less than ½ yard of fabric, so you can splurge on something extravagant without spending a fortune. My favorite pastime is finding fabric at garage sales and in remnant bins; I also save old garments, drapes, and other fabric items, if I like the fabric's look or feel. Don't be afraid to mix and match utilitarian with decorator fabrics; if you think the fabric is beautiful, practical, and durable enough for its intended function, go for it!

Purchasing and Caring for Fabric

The best place to look for these practical fabrics is your local fabric store. Most fabric stores stock basic cheesecloth (or a light-weight woven interfacing), muslin, poplin, canvas, and twill

DECORATING AND DYEING FABRIC

If you are interested in decorating or dyeing the fabric yourself, you can save some money by buying the basic unbleached canvas or twill. Just remember that paints, inks, and dyes cannot be applied to fabrics with a heavy coating on the surface. If you are using a coated or nylon fabric for functional reasons, decorate with needlework or trim, instead of paints. These may be in a separate section from the dyed varieties, so be sure to check all areas of the store.

fabrics. Basic fabrics are frequently on sale, so watch for a good deal and then buy in quantity.

There are also sewing craft mail-order catalogs that stock yardage of basic fabrics, often at very good prices (see Resource List). For synthetic sporting and outdoor fabrics, check your local fabric store; if they don't stock it, they can certainly order it for you. Recreational retailers that stock hiking and mountaineering gear, and boating supply catalogs are two other possible sources for many of the heavy-weight fabrics. Military surplus stores often carry fabrics and trims (the military has exceptionally high standards, particularly for fabrics to be used outdoors); you can even purchase surplus tents or tarps and cut them up for smaller projects. Canvas painter's drop cloths can be an inexpensive way to purchase a large piece of yardage for a lower price (a 12 x 15' drop cloth is equivalent to 20 square yards of fabric).

Storing Your Fabric

When you work often with basic fabrics, you can buy them when the price is right, and save them until you are ready to sew. I keep my fabrics boxed and labeled by weight and type, such as "medium-weight paintables" and "heavy industrials," so I can find them when I need them. The only requirement is that you have a cool, dark, dry place to store your excess fabric. Colors can fade from exposure to light and heat, and even indoors, wools and cottons can absorb moisture and begin to mildew over time.

Mildew can be removed from cotton and other vegetable fibers by washing in a mild bleach solution. Don't bleach wool, however, since the bleach will eventually dissolve it. Instead, dry clean wool or use a mild solution of hydrogen peroxide, and neutralize it by rinsing in a mild vinegar solution. Many of the synthetics will resist mildew, but if they begin to take on a moldy odor, sponge them off with a mild bleach solution. Do this for fabric yardage and finished projects as well.

Preparing Your Fabric for Use

You can't really know how much a fabric will shrink until you wash it. I urge you to do so before sewing anything. Making a project prior to washing the fabric can result in tremendous disappointment if you later wash it and find that 8 percent shrinkage in the filling direction caused puckering — there is nothing you can do once the item is sewn.

If you are combining a washable fabric with a "dry clean only" fabric (like a cotton twill interior with a silk tapestry outer cover), wash both pieces of fabric separately, as recommended, and then sew the project, recognizing that after combining the two, you will need to clean the item using the gentler of the two methods from then on, since a dry-clean fabric will not withstand the washing process.

Testing for Colorfastness

Fabric dyes and inks are applied in a number of ways and utilize a myriad of chemicals. The question of colorfastness is twofold: (1) Will the color stay as it is in the unwashed fabric? and, (2) Will the color transfer onto other fabrics when I use or launder it?

Color bleeding. We've all had the experience of washing a new garment with our white underwear and ending up with underwear in shades of pink or blue. It is good practice to prewash all fabrics before using them; if there is some bleeding of color, washing the fabric by itself for the first few times usually takes care of the problem. Occasionally, a dye is so unstable that it will transfer onto skin or upholstery with or without the presence of moisture (e.g., perspiration or rain). You can test for this vulnerability by rubbing the surface of a fabric with a small piece of white cotton fabric, both dry and damp, to see if color transfers. A small amount of color transfer is common but more than a minor tinting of the cloth is unacceptable. Such fabrics have no business being on the market and should be avoided.

Color fading. Since the dye or ink on the surface of a fabric wears down over time, or from many washings, color fading is normal, particularly with printed fabrics. If you purchase fabric and notice severe fading after the first few launderings, you should return the fabric to the retailer. Some fabrics are labeled "dry clean only" because they are very prone to color fading in the wash, even though excessive shrinkage may not be a problem (as is the case with most dry-clean items).

The Savvy Fabric Shopper

If you aren't experienced at buying fabric, here are a few facts that will help you know what you're buying and how to ask for it:

✂ Fabrics are sold from bolts that contain a total of 30 to 50 yards, and are cut by the running yard, regardless of the width. Usually a minimum purchase of ¼ yard is required.

✂ Fabric is produced in several standard widths: 36 inches, 45 inches, 54 inches, and 60 inches; it's also produced in smaller or larger widths for particular uses.

✂ With most fabrics, a shrinkage rate of 0 to 8 percent is fairly common, although the rate is different for each direction of the fabric. When shrinkage in the length creeps up to and over 5 percent, you will need to purchase extra fabric to compensate. This is often the case with flannel, terrycloth and many 100 percent cotton fabrics. Severe shrinkage is a legitimate reason to return fabric to the store, or you may decide to calculate the lost yardage and buy more to compensate. I make a point of telling the fabric store of my experiences so they can warn other customers of the shrinkage issue.

✂ The finished edges of the fabric are called selvages, and are usually thicker than the rest of the fabric. With most projects, you will need to start cutting inside the selvages. This means that a 45-inch wide fabric may have only 44 inches of working fabric. If you can use the selvage as your seam allowance, by all means do so.

✂ Most fabrics have a face and a back side. When on the bolt, the face of the fabric is turned to the inside to protect it, so fabric stores usually flip over the end of the fabric to display the face. For printed or brushed fabrics, the face is obvious; with many other fabrics, it is really a matter of personal preference which side you choose to use as the face. Be sure to examine both sides of the fabric before you buy it.

✂ Most fabrics sold on bolts have laundering instructions printed on the bolt end; be sure to read these before you buy and write down the instructions if you want to remember them. For the projects in this book, you generally want to use fabrics that are machine washable.

✂ If you are making an item that will need to be laundered, but will be difficult to iron due to its construction, (many pockets or layers of fabric, several fabrics mixed together in the same item, etc.), then you need to be aware of how wrinkle resistant the fabric is. Even though we all love natural fibers, there are times when using wrinkle-resistant synthetics makes more sense.

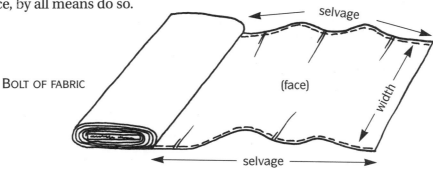

BOLT OF FABRIC   (face)   selvage   width   selvage

two

Techniques & Tools for Cutting, Sewing, and Finishing

Before you dive into the projects in this book, it will be helpful for you to know how the patterns are designed and how to best use them. Although each project includes specific step-by-step instructions, many of the general sewing techniques and finishing touches recommended are described in greater detail in this chapter. Therefore, it might help to read through this chapter before beginning any project; you can then refer back to specific sections, as needed, once you've begun to sew.

Using the Patterns in This Book

As you look over different project instructions, you'll notice that most projects begin with a fairly simple cutting layout diagram. This is the optimal layout for the pattern pieces, on the length of fabric specified. However, if you're like me, you may occasionally want to use up some of the odd-shaped scraps of fabric or other remnants you happen to have on hand to make one

of these items. You may also want to add your own creative touches by using a variety of different fabrics for the same project. For these reasons, every cutting layout includes the measurements for each pattern piece, so you can measure out various pieces on different pieces of fabric, if desired.

Tips for Laying Out Pattern Pieces

Most of the layouts are pretty straightforward, without a lot of complicated folds and refolds. The following guidelines will help you avoid running into problems such as pieces that don't look right once they're sewn together.

Preshrink all fabrics. Always preshrink your fabric to eliminate the disastrous effects of differential shrinkage between the length and width of the fabric, and between different fabrics in the same sewn item. Iron fabric flat after washing, and lay it on a flat surface, as straight as possible, before laying out the pattern.

Go with the grain. To create stability and avoid having the fabric twist as you sew, always place pattern pieces along the straight grain of the fabric, unless otherwise noted. This means that the straight edge of the pattern pieces should be parallel to either the warp or filling yarns (the length or width) of the fabric. In most of these projects, it is not overly important which direction you choose, as long as the grain is straight. Many of the fabrics suggested for these projects have obvious grain — you will be able to see the perpendicular lines of the woven yarns. If not, you can determine a grain guideline by pulling out threads along the raw edge of the fabric until you can establish one long thread running across the fabric's entire width or length.

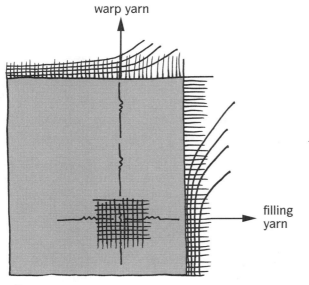

warp yarn

filling yarn

FINDING STRAIGHT GRAIN

Pay attention to the design. If the fabric you have selected has stripes, plaids, or another obvious directional pattern, decide what direction you want the pattern to be running (i.e., up and down the item, or across the width), and lay out your pieces accordingly. (See the "Buy Extra Fabric" box for other tips on working with designed fabrics.)

Keep the nap consistent. Napped, brushed, or pile fabrics have a directionality to them. You can determine whether a fabric has a nap by running your hand along the surface of the fabric in both directions. If you notice that the fabric feels smooth (with the nap) in one direction and course (against the nap) in the other direction, then you need to take this into account as you lay out your pattern pieces so that the nap is running in the same direction for all of them. A Hinged Stadium Seat (see page 122) with the nap running in one direction on the seat cushion and the opposite direction on the back cushion will look worn quickly, since, as you slide in and out of it, you will be pushing against the nap on one panel, and with it on the other, resulting in uneven wear. (See the "Buy Extra Fabric" box for other tips on working with napped fabrics.)

BUY EXTRA FABRIC

When you sew with a napped fabric, you will need to purchase extra fabric to accommodate all the pattern pieces that will need to be placed in the same direction. Likewise, if you choose a patterned fabric with obvious stripes, plaids, or motifs that need to be matched, additional fabric will be required so you can move the pattern pieces around on the fabric as needed. If you aren't familiar with undirectional placement and matching techniques, work with plain fabrics at first. Once you've had some experience using sewing patterns and understand how the pieces fit together, you will be able to visualize what pieces need to match up, and can then begin to use fabric with a nap or pattern.

Flatten the fabric. If the selvage is wavy, trim it off, and then pull threads out until you can see one long thread running the length of the fabric. If the fabric is loosely woven, you may not have to physically pull out the threads; instead, try pulling on a thread an inch or two inside the selvage to create a "pucker," a perfectly straight line running the length of the grain. Then, using this line as your grain guideline, cut and reflatten the fabric.

Transferring the Pattern Layout

When transferring a pattern layout to fabric, be sure to transfer all markings indicated on the layout and in the assembly instructions (some points are marked before cutting, others are done as you sew). In addition to the outline of the pattern pieces, there are placement points for pockets, pleats, fasteners, and other additions you will make as you sew. Use tailor's chalk (in pencil form, sharpened) for marking on the face of the fabric, and a fine-line felt-tip marker on the back of the fabric, or in the seam allowances.

There are three methods you can use to transfer the patterns shown in the project cutting layouts onto fabric. Select the technique you feel most comfortable with, or try out each one in turn to discover your preference.

Direct method. On the wrong side of the fabric (unless otherwise specified), use a metal straightedge ruler and pen to measure out and draw the dimensions of each pattern piece. Be sure to mark the points indicated for pleats, pockets, or findings.

Paper pattern. Draw the pattern pieces onto tracing paper (vellum or heavier stock) in the assigned dimensions and cut them out. Pin these pieces onto the fabric and cut around them. Mark the indicated attachment points on the paper pattern. Before removing the pinned pattern from the fabric, mark these points by stitching through both the pattern and the fabric with a basting stitch, using brightly colored thread. If markings are simple, like ½ inch seam allowances, you might prefer to use chalk to place the markings directly on the fabric.

Cardboard pattern. If I am going to make an item several times, I often drawn the pattern pieces onto cardboard to make a pattern that can be used many times. To mark key attachment points, punch holes at the appropriate spots in the cardboard and mark in chalk, pen, or with thread onto the fabric. This method works particularly well for designs with odd or difficult geometric shapes such as circles or triangles.

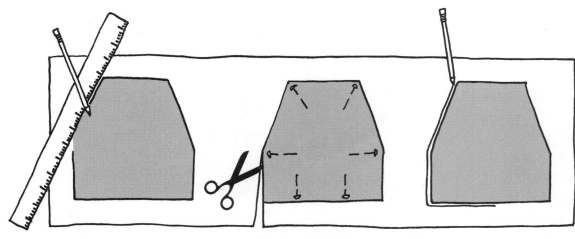

DIRECTLY ONTO FABRIC   PINNED PAPER PATTERN   TRACING AROUND CARDBOARD

Cutting Out the Pattern Pieces

Don't be afraid to cut fabric. Do what all good carpenters do — measure twice, cut once. When you have completely transferred the pattern pieces and all markings onto the fabric, (including the pattern piece identification labels, so you don't get confused about what piece it is later), use a sharp cutting tool and carefully cut out the pieces.

In many of the projects, especially those with rounded corners, the pattern pieces are sized slightly larger than needed, to allow for trimming later. When several layers are going to be sewn together into a rounded corner, it is easier to trim all of the pieces after they have been stitched together.

Sewing Terms and Techniques

The projects in this book require an understanding of only basic techniques and terminology. If you're a beginner or haven't used a sewing machine for some time, the following review of basic terms and techniques should be helpful. Even if you're an experienced sewer, you may find some interesting tips here that you haven't tried before.

Seam Allowances

The seam allowances for these projects are not a consistent ⅝ inch, as in most commercial patterns, because such a large seam allowance is excessive for many smaller items. Therefore, be sure to read the step-by-step instructions carefully for seam allowance guidelines. The most common ones used are ⅛, ¼, and ½ inch.

Seam allowance is measured from the machine needle to the edge of the fabric. Set up whatever guidelines you need on your machine to make it easy to maintain standard seam allowances. On my machine, I placed a strip of masking tape on the needle plate at exactly ½ inch from the needle. With this guide, I can easily align the edge of my fabric with the edge of the tape. I also know that my standard presser foot extends ⅛ inch from the needle, so when I align the fabric perfectly with the edge of the foot, I obtain a seam allowance of ⅛ inch.

MARKING ROUNDED CORNERS

Rounded corners are aesthetically pleasing and allow bias binding (see page 27) to be attached in a flat, continuous length. To create the sewing line for a rounded corner, first draw the perpendicular lines that form a square corner. Measure and mark points 1 ½ inches from the corners. Connect these points by drawing a smooth curve from one point to the next, around the corner, evening out the curve by eye or by using a french curve (a flexible tool available in a sewing store). Create this same curved shape for all the corners on the project.

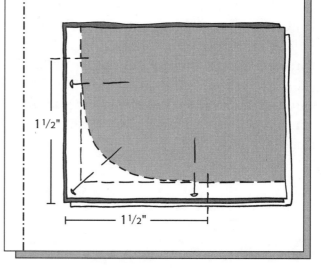

Stitching Types and Techniques

Most of the sewing in this book uses a simple, straight lock stitch, the standard stitch on a machine. (It's called a lock stitch because the top and bottom threads meet between the layers of the fabric, and are "locked" together to form each stitch.) For a standard seam, your stitch width should be set at 10 to 12 stitches per inch (spi). You can check the accuracy of your machine setting by placing a ruler along a sewn seam and counting the loops per inch. For machine basting, adjust the width to 6 to 8 stitches per inch.

When sewing, be sure to adjust the thread tensions so that both sides of the stitch are slightly looped. If one side looks like a straight thread running along the surface, and the other side is very looped, the tension is off. If the problem (looped thread) is on the top of the fabric, adjust the tension for the bobbin. If the problem is on the bottom of the fabric, adjust the upper tension. (See page 4, for more on tension.)

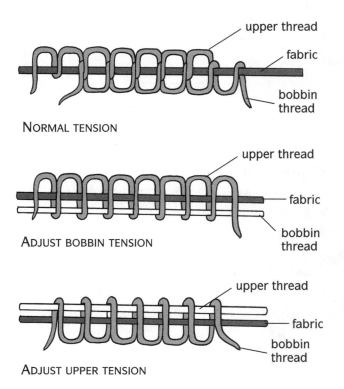

NORMAL TENSION

ADJUST BOBBIN TENSION

ADJUST UPPER TENSION

Serge and zigzag stitches. I do not refer to serge or zigzag stitching in the project instructions, but either can be used for finishing fabric edges. If a project calls for turning the edge under ¼ inch, and then ½ inch for a hem, you can serge or zigzag the raw edge ¼ inch first. Then you can easily turn under the stitched edge of fabric, which is of a consistent ¼ inch width. (A *serger* is a three- or four-thread sewing machine that produces a stitch, called an *overedge* or *overlock stitch*, that loops around the edge of the fabric.) You can also use a zigzag stitch for a decorative effect when topstitching. On most machines, this just requires changing the presser foot to one with a wide slot for the needle to move back and forth, and changing the machine setting from straight to zigzag stitching.

If you are an experienced sewer and wish to modify the patterns for the serger, be aware that you will have to change many of the seam allowances to adapt to the narrower width of the serged seam allowance.

Hand stitching. Some of the projects call for hand stitching or basting. A slip stitch is used to fasten one layer to another. To make it invisible on the face of the fabric, catch only the back of a thread on the main fabric piece when fastening a hem or fabric layer in place. Basting is a simple running stitch that is removed later. Stitching at ¼ inch intervals will hold most pieces securely in place.

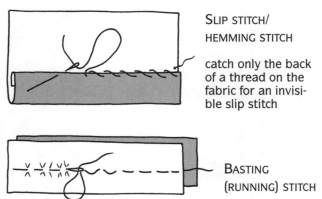

SLIP STITCH/
HEMMING STITCH

catch only the back of a thread on the fabric for an invisible slip stitch

BASTING
(RUNNING) STITCH

Stitching around corners. To make a clean, angled corner, keep your seam allowance exact and stop the needle (preferably when down into the fabric) at the precise point where the corner seam allowance for the adjoining edge begins. (To be exact, mark this point, before you begin sewing the first edge.) Raise the presser foot and pivot the fabric so that the presser foot is pointing down the next edge. Lower the presser foot and resume sewing.

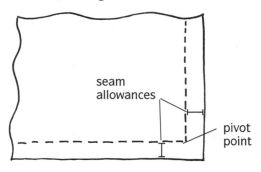

seam
allowances

pivot
point

Backstitching. At the start and finish of seams, stitch forward, then back, then forward again, about three stitches, to lock the start and end of the seam in place and prevent it from pulling out. Backstitch several times at high-stress areas (e.g., on pockets, straps, handles, and any place that will be stressed when in use). Do not backstitch on basted seams.

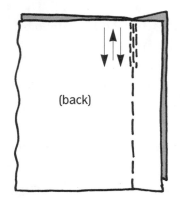

(back)

Topstitching. Topstitching is a simple lock stitch on the face of the fabric, placed at a certain distance from the fabric edge. It is used for stability (to prevent stretch), security (to prevent seam failure by securing the seam allowance or other layers of fabric to each other), and decoration. Often, one or more rows of topstitching will be specified in a project. Keep them straight and at the specified distance from each other for a professional look.

Box stitch. The box stitch is a reinforcing configuration that is used in high-stress areas such as strap/handle joins, or for attaching buckles and hooks to lengths of twill tape or strap webbing. To begin, stitch around the periphery of a square or rectangular area, attaching whatever components are specified in the project. Then, point the presser foot diagonally across the square, and run a line of stitching. Stitch along the top side of the square to the opposite corner, and then run another diagonal line of stitching to form an X inside the box. When you get to the corner, turn and stitch along the bottom edge of the square, and backstitch at the end.

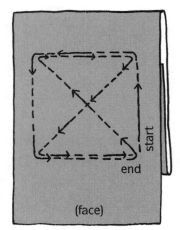

start

end

(face)

Forming Seams

Seams are the basis of all sewn construction. They bind together two or more layers of fabric. Here are two commonly used seam types.

Plain seam. To stitch a plain seam, place two pieces of fabric together (generally with right sides facing and edges even), and, using the seam allowance specified, stitch through the two layers. To press and set the seam, press it flat first as it has been stitched, then open it and press the seam allowances apart.

Felled seam. For applications in which a clean finish is needed on both sides of the fabric and a very strong seam is required (e.g., on your blue jeans), a felled seam is used. To create a felled seam, first stitch a seam using at least ½-inch seam allowance. Trim one side of the seam allowance to half its original width. Fold the longer seam allowance over and under the trimmed one, and topstitch the folded edge of the sandwiched seam allowance to the main fabric piece. This will conceal all of the raw edges and strengthen the seam by securing it a second time. To further eliminate bulk, you can run a second row of topstitching along the inner edge of the felled folds closest to the seam.

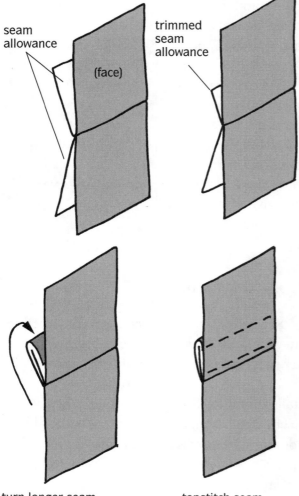

seam allowance

trimmed seam allowance

(face)

turn longer seam allowance around shorter

topstitch seam allowance down

Hemming

A hem is a clean-finished edge formed by folding the fabric twice toward the back side of the fabric, to conceal all of the raw edges, and stitching along the inner edge to hold the folded fabric in place. Straight and even hems are most easily achieved through careful, measured ironing before sewing. You can either premark the fabric before you iron or measure as you iron. To premark the fabric, measure in from the edge the desired distance for the first fold, and make a line or a series of dots, in chalk, on the face of the fabric (marking on the wrong side of the fabric doesn't work well, since you will be folding over your marks). Do the same for the second fold. Press (toward the back of the fabric) along the first fold line, and then the second. Pin the hem in place. To complete the hem stitch along the inner fold, by hand (using a slip stitch) or by machine per the instructions given. Some hems are double topstitched, to flatten the outer edge, and create a decorative effect.

Mitering Corners

For a mitered hem, fold and press the first fold of the hem (½ inch) toward the back of the fabric. Press the second fold of the hem (1 inch) toward the face of the fabric. Diagonally fold in and press the corner. Open out the pressed edges, and refold the corner right sides together with the raw edges even to define the diagonal, and center the diagonal from both edges. Stitch along the diagonally pressed line. Open out the corner seam, clip the corner seam allowance to ½ inch, and press it open. Turn the corner toward the back of the fabric and press.

For mitering trim around a corner, stitch the outside edge of the the trim down the full length of the project. Next, stitch the inside edge of the trim, stopping at the pivot point of the corner (one seam allowance away from the other edge). Fold the remaining trim back over itself so that the fold is even with the raw edge of the fabric. Stitch the diagonal line that runs from the outer to the inner corner of the trim. Pivot the trim around the corner and continue sewing it to the

MITERING CORNERS

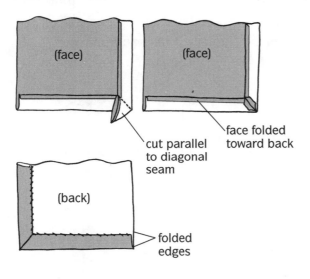

cut parallel to diagonal seam

face folded toward back

folded edges

MITERING TRIM

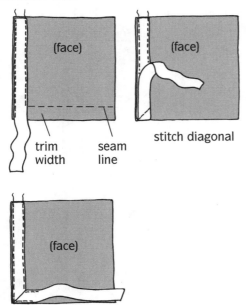

trim width   seam line

stitch diagonal

fabric. Pivots, corners, and miters take up more trim than you might think. Do *not* precut the trim length. Start with plenty of trim, and complete the entire outer edge before clipping.

Making Casings

Casings are created like topstitched hems but are designed to enclose elastic (or other items, such as a drawstring). The width of the casing and the distance between the rows of topstitching are critical, since you must be able to pull the elastic through the casing, and have enough room around the elastic to allow the fabric to gather. Pay particular attention to the measurements noted in the project instructions; if you change the size of the elastic, be sure to modify the casing size to accommodate the change.

Once a casing is sewn, you will have to insert the elastic (or drawstring). Attach a safety pin that will fit inside the casing to one end of the elastic and push the pin through and around the inside of the casing. Pin the other end of the elastic to the fabric, so that it does not pull through the casing. Stitch or tie the two ends of the elastic (or drawstring) together, as directed in the project instructions.

Making Gathers

To produce gathers, loose lines of stitching are sewn and the thread ends are then pulled to create small folds in the fabric. Gathers are used to produce fullness in an area of fabric. In this book, they are also used to make "puffed" pockets or three-dimensional stuffed shapes.

To gather fabric, stitch along the seam line and again ¼ inch closer to the fabric edge. You can hand baste these stitching lines, or use a basting stitch on your machine (you may need to loosen the upper thread tension to allow the bobbin thread to pull easily when you make the gathers). Use strong thread to prevent breakage. The stitch length you choose will depend on how small you want the gathered folds to be (usually 2–5 stitches per inch for hand basting, and 6–8 for machine basting).

After you have completed both lines of stitching, pull the threads from one end (being careful not to pull them out at the other end), until the edge of the fabric is the desired length, if you are fitting it to another piece, and/or has the desired degree of gathers. Once you have arranged the gathers so that they are evenly spaced, stitch the gathered edge of fabric to its adjoining piece of fabric, making sure you catch all the gathers in the seam line.

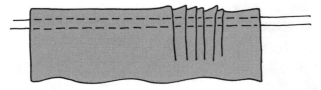

GATHERS

Forming Pleats

Pleats are accurately measured, pressed, and stitched folds that give fullness to a piece of fabric. When making pleats, there are fold lines and placement lines. You may find it helpful to mark them in different colors. A *fold line* is a line that will be folded; a *placement line* is the line that the fold will be placed against. The pleats in this book are very simple pocket pleats, which are used to form pockets that hold more than flat pockets. Much more complex pleat detail is used in dressmaking and draperies. There are four standard types of pleats: knife, box, inverted, and accordian.

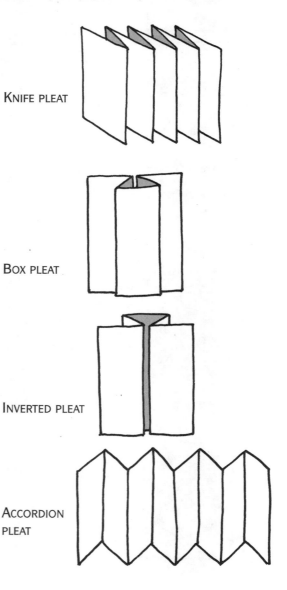

KNIFE PLEAT

BOX PLEAT

INVERTED PLEAT

ACCORDION PLEAT

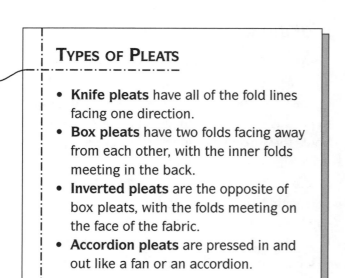

TYPES OF PLEATS

- **Knife pleats** have all of the fold lines facing one direction.
- **Box pleats** have two folds facing away from each other, with the inner folds meeting in the back.
- **Inverted pleats** are the opposite of box pleats, with the folds meeting on the face of the fabric.
- **Accordion pleats** are pressed in and out like a fan or an accordion.

Trims, Fasteners, Findings, and Fillings

Selecting and adding trims, fasteners, findings, and other finishing touches to your projects can be a great way to express your creativity. These items can add a lot to both the look and the functionality of your finished project. The search for these items is half the fun: To find unique items, try rummaging through sewing notions departments, sporting goods and hardware stores, and odds-and-ends boxes at yard sales. Make sure that these additions will last as long as the fabric and construction of the project, and can stand up to their intended use. Following are a few guidelines for choosing wisely, as well as for using these items to modify projects so that they fit a specific need or function.

Bias Binding Tape

Bias binding tape is a strip of fabric, cut on the bias (on a diagonal of 45 degrees from the selvage), and pressed under to create a finished edge. When fabric is cut on the bias, it has greater stretch and will bend easily to fit around curves. Bias binding allows you to clean-finish an edge of fabric without doubling or tripling the thickness with repeated folding (as in hemming). For small-scale projects, bias tapes are sold in 4-yard packages and in a multitude of colors and widths. For larger projects, or if you just want to have a supply on hand, it can be purchased in 100-yard rolls.

Before applying bias binding, always trim the seam allowances smaller than the folded width of the binding; the binding must cover the entire seam allowance and be stitched to the base fabric exactly on the outline of the pattern piece. There are two types of bias binding: single-fold and double-fold.

Single-fold bias binding. This is bias binding that is turned under once along each edge. There are several methods for applying it, all of which entail two sewing steps.

- **Method 1:** No stitch line on fabric face. Open out the fold of the bias tape along one edge of the binding, and place this edge along the edge of the fabric, right sides facing. Stitch along the unfolded crease. Now bring the folded side of the binding over the edges of the fabric and binding, and hand stitch it in place.

- **Method 2:** Stitch line along edge of binding. Stitch the binding to the face of the fabric as in Method 1. Pull the folded side of the binding over the edges of the fabric and binding, so that the fold of the bias tape covers the stitch line. On the front of the fabric, stitch "in the ditch" right along the outer edge of the binding, on the fabric itself, catching the edge of the binding along the back.

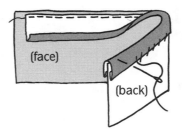

single-fold bias binding

double-fold bias binding

METHOD 1

Unfold — machine stitch — turn — hand stitch

METHOD 2

Unfold — machine stitch — turn — machine topstitch

(face)   (back)

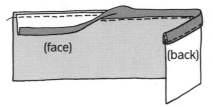

MAKING BIAS BINDING

You can make your own binding from matching or contrasting fabrics. Start with a piece of fabric cut on the straight grain. Fold it on the diagonal, lining up the length and width grains, to find the true bias.

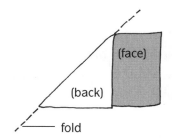

Press and unfold the fabric. Then mark several strips of the desired width (see below) along the bias, following the true bias line, and cut along these lines.

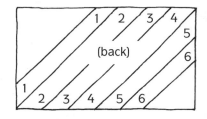

With right sides together, place one end of one bias strip at a right angle to the next and stitch along this line (the straight grain) to connect the two lengths.

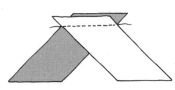

This creates a mitered (diagonal) join seam. Repeat with the remaining strips to make one strip of the desired length. Whenever possible, start with a length of binding longer than you need to complete the project edge, so that you do not have to join a new length while you are binding.

Cut bias strips four times the desired width of the finished trim (e.g., for a 1/2-inch tape, cut the strips 2 inches wide). Press under 1/2 inch along both outer edges. Then, press the strip in half lengthwise so that one side is slightly wider (1/16 inch) than the other. There is also a tool available that turns and folds the fabric strips; you feed them through a curved metal shape of the size desired, after which you press the folds in place. This metal tool is available at sewing, fabric, and craft stores in different sizes: 1/2 inch and 1 inch are the most common.

An easier way to make long lengths of bias binding is to make one **continuous strip of bias binding.** Follow the instructions for making bias binding, but instead of cutting the fabric into individual strips, fold the fabric to connect the lines, offsetting by one strip width, as shown, and sew a seam along the straight grain to connect the two fabric edges. (Essentially, you are sewing all of the strips together at once, instead of cutting them and connecting them separately.) Begin cutting the offset strip at one end, and continue cutting around the circular piece of fabric along the marked strip lines, to make one continuous length of bias binding. Press the bias binding edges to make either a single- or double-fold binding.

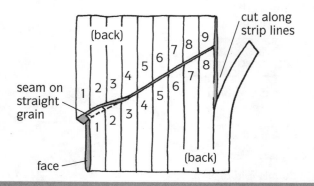

- **Method 3:** Topstitched binding. Keeping both edges of the binding folded, place the wrong side of the bias tape against the face of the fabric and topstitch along the folded edge. Bring the other folded bias edge over and around the fabric edge, and hand stitch it to the back of the fabric.

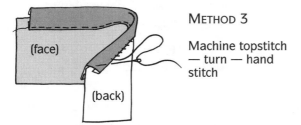

METHOD 3

Machine topstitch — turn — hand stitch

(face)

(back)

Ribbons and tapes with finished edges (e.g., grosgrain ribbon, twill tape, and other flat woven-edged trims) can be substituted for single-fold bias binding. However, they can only be used on straight edges; since they are not cut on the bias, they will twist if used on curved shapes. Before sewing them to the fabric, press a crease slightly off center. Then use according to one of the three methods described or apply like double-fold bias binding.

Double-fold bias binding. Both edges of double-fold binding are folded under, and then the tape is folded a second time. To apply, place the off-center fold over the edge of the fabric with the slightly wider side of the bias tape placed against the back of the fabric. Then topstitch close to the edges of the bias tape through all layers with the fabric face up. Placing the slightly wider side of the bias tape in back ensures that you will catch it in the stitch line. Some people find it helpful to use a zipper foot when topstitching the binding,

to hold it in place. If you don't want a topstitched "look," you can apply double-fold bias tape using any of the three methods described for attaching single-fold binding.

Adding bias trim with a mitered join. If you run out of binding while you are sewing, you can add another length of binding, using a mitered join. Stop stitching within 2 inches of the joining spot. Open up the folds of both the sewn binding and the piece you are adding. Place them at right angles to each other, right sides facing, so that when you stitch them together along the straight grain, they will form a straight, continuous length of binding.

Finishing bias ends with a lapped finish. Trim the starting end of the binding along the straight grain (this will be on the diagonal to the length of the binding). When you begin binding, leave about ½ inch from this raw edge unsewn; this will help you line up the binding ends. As you bind an item and come back around to the starting point, stop sewing about 1 inch from the starting point (the raw edge of the binding). Keep the needle in the fabric as you prepare the ends. Trim the end of the binding on the straight grain, leaving enough length to turn under a ¼-inch hem and still cover the raw edge of the binding at the starting point. Pin the finished edge over the raw edge, and continue stitching the binding in place, lining both pieces up carefully. Slip stitch the turned edge of the binding end to the underlayer, if desired.

ATTACHING DOUBLE-FOLD BINDING

piece of fabric being bound

back is 1/16" wider than front to ensure catching in seam

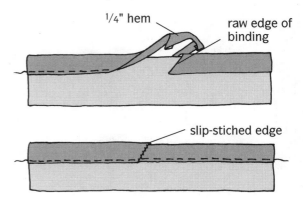

1/4" hem

raw edge of binding

slip-stiched edge

Binding corners. I generally design items bound by double-fold bias with rounded corners, to eliminate the need for mitering. However, you can bind angled corners if you use single-fold binding and miter the corners. To miter on an outer corner, stitch the binding, right sides facing, along one side. Stop stitching and backstitch at the pivot point of the corner (one seam allowance away from the edge), leaving the needle down. Pivot around the corner to the next side of the fabric and continue stitching the binding down along the new edge (this will cause a "pucker" in the bias binding at the corner). When you have sewn the periphery of the fabric piece with binding, fold the binding around to the back of the fabric. Miter the corners by folding in one side of the binding and pinning the diagonal at each corner, before folding in the next side of binding. Stitch the back of the binding down as you would normally. Slip stitch the mitered corner join.

MITERED CORNER BINDING

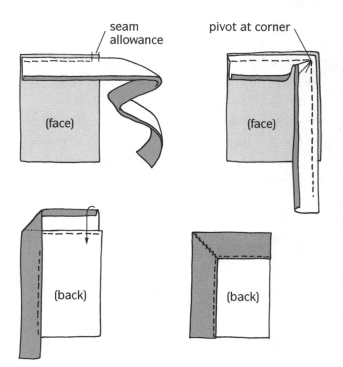

Twill Tape

Twill tape is a flat, narrow trim woven with a twill weave — you can see the telltale twill diagonal wales (or herringbone pattern) on the surface of the tape. It is available in a variety of widths and weights and is made of cotton or nylon. Twill tape is durable and useful in many applications: It can be used as a seam edge finish, as loops or straps, or to stabilize a seam. Light-weight twill tape is often used to bind the edges of rugs; heavy-weight nylon twill tape is commonly used for handles. The combination of the nylon fiber and the twill weave produces incredible strength and is actually similar to the strap webbing discussed in the next section.

Strap Webbing

This material is a narrow woven cotton or nylon trim that comes in many widths. It has many uses. For the projects in this book, I use it frequently for straps and handles; it can also be sewn around the weight-bearing surfaces of a bag, to help take the stress off the stitching, and allow you to carry heavier loads without breaking the seams. When used in conjunction with D rings and buckles, this product also makes an excellent belt for aprons.

Ribbon

If you decide to make some of the lighter-duty projects, you may choose to use ribbon instead of heavy tapes for ties and trimming. I recommend that you use grosgrain ribbon — a woven ribbon that has visible crosswise ribs and is stronger than many of the thin synthetic ribbons. It is available in a variety of widths and colors, and can be used in many of the same applications as bias tape.

Drawstrings

In various applications, you may need to use cord for drawstrings. Nylon cord is sold by the yard and in shorter lengths with finished ends. As an alternative, consider using the waist drawstring from an old ski jacket, or the leather laces you've had around for years.

Elastic

Elastics come in many widths and have abundant uses. The degree of tension needed to stretch different elastics varies, so it is best to test different types before purchasing, to see which elastic most suits your needs. Read the roll labels to see if they indicate intended uses. Nonroll elastics work well in casings for waistbands — they stay flat even after repeated washings and will not twist up inside the casing. Some elastics have a built-in drawstring. This elastic is used in waistbands; however, you can also use it in the casing of a bag. Due to the elastic, the bag will cinch up naturally; the drawstring allows you to seal it even tighter manually, so nothing falls out.

Welting

Welting, or piping cord, is the internal material that stiffens a piped seam. It is most often seen in upholstery. The cord is encased in a fabric sleeve of fabric (usually bias cut), which is then used to trim the edges of seams. This provides stability and protects the seam from abrasion.

Welting comes in different fiber contents (cotton, polyester, jute, and plastic), and thicknesses. The thickness you choose depends on the end use of the project you are making; the thicker the cord, the more prominent the welt will be; and the thicker the fabric, the thicker you will probably want the welting to be.

Making welting. To make welting, you first need to make a length of bias binding (see box, page 28). Fold the bias binding in half over cord of the desired diameter. Using a zipper foot, stitch the fabric closed around the cord. The seam line does not have to be flush with the cord — in fact, leaving ⅛ inch to ³⁄₁₆ inch of space is preferable, so that when you attach the piping to your fabric pieces, you can stitch very close to the cord and the first stitch line will not show. Trim the seam allowance of the welting to ½ inch.

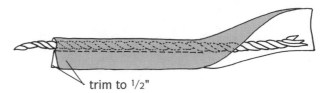

trim to ½"

Attaching welting. Trim the raw edges of the welting so that it is the same width as your seam allowance. Lay the welting on the right side of the fabric, lining up the raw edges. (In general, piping is first stitched to the most prominent piece of fabric, such as the front of a pillow, and then to the back or side panels.) Using a zipper foot, stitch over or just inside (closer to the welt cord) the seam line that enclosed the cord bias binding. Now pin the second layer of fabric to the piped piece of fabric, right sides together. With the presewn piece facing up, stitch *as close to the piping* as possible (this seam, tightly wedged between the piping seam and the actual cord, tightens the cord in the casing and sandwiches the piping between the two pieces of fabric to form the piped edge).

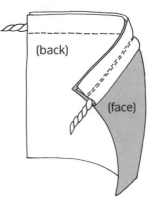

(back)

(face)

Finishing welting ends. Use this method to join the ends of welting, making sure that when you begin binding you leave a tail long enough to join another piece (approximately 6 to 8 inches). When you stitch around the item, return to 6 inches from starting point. Lay the weltings alongside each other, and mark in chalk on both pieces, the center of the point where they overlap. Unstitch and remove the welting cord. Lay the fabrics at right angles, pin the chalk marks to each other exactly, and stitch along the straight grain right over the chalk mark. When you open out the welting, it will be the exact length to finish binding the piece, seamed perfectly to fit. Trim the welting cord so that the two ends meet, and stitch the welting to the fabric, encasing the cord at the same time.

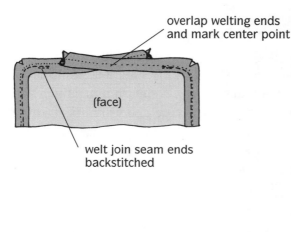

overlap welting ends and mark center point

(face)

welt join seam ends backstitched

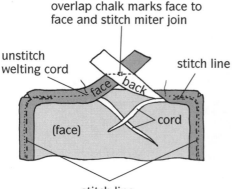

overlap chalk marks face to face and stitch miter join

unstitch welting cord

stitch line

face back

(face)

cord

stitch line

Snaps

Snaps (or "grippers") are fasteners that have two halves — the ball and the socket — that join together securely. Light-weight sew-on snaps are used on light- to medium-weight fabrics and in several applications, including holding down pocket flaps and securing tabs over zippers. Stitch them onto items so that the socket piece is anchored (as on a pocket), and the ball piece is located on the flap, so it can be pushed into the socket.

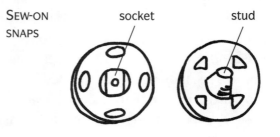

SEW-ON SNAPS   socket   stud

Heavy-duty snaps, which are available in several sizes and decorative designs, are attached with a hammer and metal die or with special pliers. There are four parts to these snaps: the cap prong, which attaches to the stud (ball); and the ring prong, which attaches to the socket. The two-part construction of each snap half is sandwiched around the fabric to form a tight bond, similar to a rivet. Because these metal snaps are so strong, the fabric must be strong enough to withstand the pulling required to release the snap — often, two layers of fabric and interfacing are required. All four-part snaps come with instructions. If you have never purchased them before, be sure to buy a package that comes with the metal die. After that, you will only need to buy refill packs.

To attach these snaps, place the cap prong, with points facing up, on a protected surface. Lay the fabric on the prong, right side down, and push the points up through the fabric. Now place the stud over the fabric, so that the prongs are lined up in the stud holes. Position the die on top of this layered setup, and hammer until the prongs bend over and grasp the stud. Repeat this process with the ring prong and socket, so that the stud and socket will meet between the two layers of fabric.

FOUR-PART SNAPS

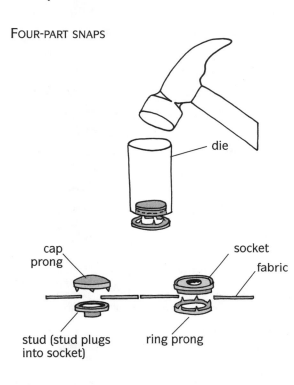

RECYCLING USED FINDINGS AND FASTENERS

Before I discard any belt, bag, or other item with metal findings, I remove the functional parts and save them. They come in handy when I'm feeling creative and don't want to go shopping. Don't overlook anything! Even the little white buckles on your lingerie straps can be reused in another project. "Free" boxes at yard sales are also a great source of findings. Don't be afraid to let your imagination run wild; mix and match fasteners to add a funky or artistic look to your item.

Grommets and Eyelets

These metal findings form a stable hole in the fabric, to allow drawstrings to pull through without abrading the fabric. Grommets and eyelets have two parts: a pronged washer and a tube-shaped piece (also called an *eyelet*), which is bent over to further reinforce the join. They come in many sizes, and are also available in plastic; I found them in the camping supply section of my local hardware store. Grommets and eyelets are used for bag closures, tarp and hammock lacing, vent holes in airtight fabrications, and at times, as decoration.

Before attaching, it is wise to reinforce the fabric with a layer or two of interfacing or canvas under the grommets — they tend to pull out over time, because they are used in high-stress applications. The method of attachment is similar to snaps, but you first have to cut a hole in the fabric: Trace around the center hole of the grommet or eyelet, and then carefully clip the hole from the fabric. Slip the tube-shaped piece into the hole. Position the pronged washer on top, and place the metal die into the tube. Hammer until the tube and prongs have bent over securely.

GROMMETS

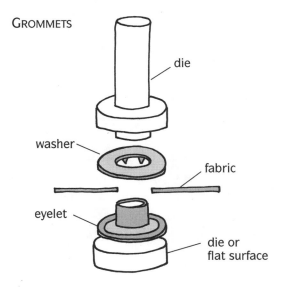

Zippers

Zippers are versatile and practical in many applications. Some are designed to be invisible, others are meant to be an integral part of the design. They consist of teeth, tape, stops, a slider, and a pull tab. A zipper generally has a top stop, which prevents the slider from pulling off at the top end of the teeth, and a bottom stop, which stops the tab from pulling off at the bottom. Some zippers are closed with a zipper stop at both ends, while others have a slider that enables them to zip in both directions. Zippers can be found in every length, from 4 inches to continuous yardage that can be cut to your specification; and are available in nylon (coil), plastic, and metal (teeth) in a variety of weights. Often, the cloth zipper tape has a raised guideline for stitch line placement.

Choosing the correct zipper depends on the fabric and end use you have in mind. Zippers with plastic teeth are great for outdoor applications; metal teeth are durable and may be preferable for upholstery projects; and nylon or light-duty plastic zippers work well for pocket and bag closures.

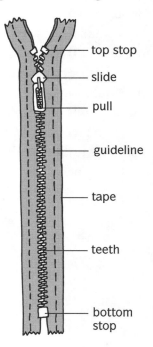

top stop
slide
pull
guideline
tape
teeth
bottom stop

Attaching zippers. Zippers are easy to insert, as long as you have a zipper foot for your sewing machine. There are many different methods; the one you choose will depend on the type of garment or item being sewn. For the projects in this book, there are two main methods.

- **Method 1:** Centered on the seam. When sewing a seam in which a zipper is to be inserted, you will need to adjust the stitches per inch as you sew the seam. Machine baste the portion of the seam that will house the zipper, and sew the rest of the seam with standard stitches per inch, making sure to backstitch at the beginning and the end of the standard seam lines. Press the seam allowances open. Pin or hand baste the zipper to the fabric, with the right side of the zipper facing the wrong side of the fabric, the teeth directly aligned over the basted stitching. When using a zipper foot, position it so that the foot is on the flat fabric, and the needle is closest to the zipper teeth. Start sewing at the top of the zipper, and stitch down its length, keeping the stitches at least ⅛ inch away from the teeth. Stitch along the raised guideline woven into the zipper tape, if there is one.

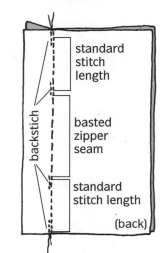

standard stitch length

backstitch

basted zipper seam

standard stitch length

(back)

Now readjust the zipper foot so that you can stitch from the top down on the other side of the zipper, with the zipper facing you. Then pivot around the bottom corner to create a seam that runs across the bottom of the zipper and meets the first seam. Backstitch over this bottom seam at least once. Using a seam ripper, open up the machine-basted portion of the seam (over the zipper). The folded edges of the fabric will perfectly conceal the zipper.

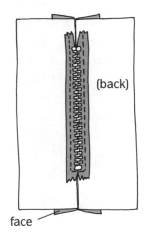

(back)

face

• **Method 2:** Stitching one side at a time. For heavier fabrics, or for zippers located along curved or pivoted seams, you will want to stitch each side of the zipper to the fabric separately. This gives added control and allows you to see the seam on the zipper face as you sew. You can separate the two pieces of fabric to expose the zipper, or move them close together to meet at the center and conceal the zipper.

To center the zipper between the fabric, turn under and press ½ inch along the edge of each piece of fabric. Open the zipper and hand baste or pin both sides of the zipper to the two pieces of fabric, right sides together, carefully lining up the turned edge of the fabric pieces with the center of the teeth. Stitch along one side of the zipper tape, at least ⅛ inch away from the teeth. Repeat for the other side. Stitch across the bottom of the zipper, just below the bottom stop, back and forth at least twice. With this method, you are essentially topstitching the zipper in place.

To offset the fabric from the teeth (to create a flap over the zipper, for example), line up the edge of the fabric with the edge of the zipper tape, right sides facing and, stitch the fabric to the zipper. Press the fabric to lap over the zipper as much or as little as your design demands, and then back over itself to create a doubled flap. Stitch through both layers of fabric to the zipper, to create a lapped zipper cover. You can topstitch it and/or edge stitch the flap along the fold. The other half of the zipper is attached to a different piece of fabric using method 2 (see above).

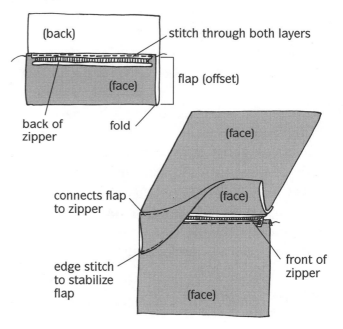

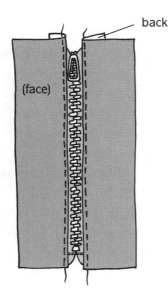

SHORTENING ZIPPERS

If you don't have a zipper of the exact length you need, fear not. Zippers can be easily shortened by hand stitching several times over the teeth at the point you wish the new zipper stop to be located. Then, you can either sew in an eye (one half of a hook-and-eye set) or bend in a new zipper stop. Cut off the remaining end of the zipper, leaving at least ¹/₂ inch below the new stop.

Hook and Loop (Velcro)

Hook and loop is a great advance in the fastener field, and often replaces zippers. It comes in many widths and colors, and is available in several quality levels. The kind with peel-and-stick glue on the back is lighter weight than the sew-in type, and can often wear out or tear. Since you will be sewing it onto fabric, make sure you choose a type with a good stable backing that can be sewn through with heavy-duty thread. Purchasing hook and loop by the yard is less expensive than in premeasured packages; if you use a lot, purchase it in rolls.

When applying hook and loop, stitch close to the edge around the periphery of both pieces. Don't worry about sewing right over the hook or loop — it will not affect the functioning of the fastener. The hook side (the rougher, coarser side) should always be placed on the fabric surface that is least likely to come into contact with other things that it might adhere to. The repeated action of pulling hook and loop open requires that you secure all of its edges; you may want to sew a second row of stitches around the hook and loop pieces to reinforce the seam.

Other Findings and Fasteners

Buckles. Although traditional prong-type buckles are used in a few projects in this book, plastic snap buckles are preferred for most outdoor applications. They are easier to fasten, do not rely on the hole in the fabric to hold them, and, because they are molded, are less likely to break under pressure. Buckles come in several styles and sizes — the width of the buckle determines the width of the strap webbing or twill tape used. To make an adjustable strap, include a slider buckle for the strap to run in and out of.

D rings. A D-ring is a metal loop shaped like the letter D. A single D ring makes a good anchor for attaching straps. Double D rings can be used like buckles. By lacing the belt through both loops, and back through a single loop, the belt becomes tensioned between the two.

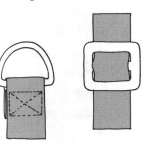

Toggle clamps/cord locks. These plastic fasteners are spring-loaded barrels that hold a drawstring tight, and are typically used on stuff sacks and garments. They are handy for camping gear and eliminate the need to make complex knots in order to keep a cord pulled tight. Toggle clamps are available at most fabric stores, or you can find them at sporting goods and recreational equipment suppliers.

Snap hooks and spring hooks. Snap hooks and spring hooks are sewn onto a loop of webbing; the hook end is used to attach the webbing to a D ring or any other type of loop. They can be sewn to a bag, and used as a hook to hold your keys for safekeeping. A spring hook has a spring-loaded lever that is pulled to release the hook; a snap hook has a piece of flexible metal that slides out of the way when pushed onto a ring, and snaps back into place when past the ring. Both types are available in rigid and swivel styles. Light-duty hooks can be found in fabric and craft stores; heavy-duty spring and snap hooks are available at many hardware stores.

snap hook   spring hook

Stiffeners

Sometimes internal layers of stiffer material are needed to reinforce or make rigid a part of an item. Stiffeners come in many varieties, thicknesses, and varying degrees of rigidity.

Interfacing. This extra layer of material is used to stiffen or reinforce areas that might otherwise be too flimsy. Interfacing comes in many weights and is generally divided into two categories: woven and nonwoven. Interfacing can be sewn or fused. Sewn interfacing is stitched onto the fabric, after which the seam allowance is trimmed close to the seam. Fusible interfacing is bonded to the fabric with an iron. Follow the manufacturer's instructions for temperature, time, and technique for fusing. When using fusible interfacing, cut the interfacing to fit inside the seam allowances of the outer piece, so that it does not add unwanted bulk to the seams.

Bolt ends of interfacing indicate what applications best suit the particular product. For the projects in this book, interfacing is used to reinforce a fabric or to stiffen and thicken an area where you want to attach a metal finding. Light-weight woven interfacing fabric can often be substituted for cheesecloth in many projects.

Cardboard and buckram. In some projects, rigidity is desired. If you are making an item that will never be washed, you can sandwich stiff cardboard between fabric to reinforce an area. Buckram is a fabric that is stiffened with starches. While it will soften some in the wash, it can be laundered. Buckram is used in the visors of baseball caps and can be formed into curved shapes.

Fillings

Fillings add a cushiony quality to your projects, to increase comfort or fill an area to create a three-dimensional shape.

Batting. Batting is a fluffy mass of fibers held together by natural tangling, heat, or resins. There are many types of flat batting available on the market, made in many thickneses, densities, and a variety of materials. Polyester is the most common, but cotton is also available. You can also buy batting that has been laminated to other fabrics, or quilted with fabric on both sides. The industrial upholstery field offers several more varieties.

For many applications, a simple, flat, polyester batting will work well, as long as you secure it along the seams and across any large areas, so that it will not shift and bunch up. To stuff three-dimensional shapes, you will need bulk batting. For greater warmth (e.g., in outdoor gear), you can purchase goose down, which is highly insulating. It must be enclosed in a "baffle" (an internal pouch) to prevent the feathers from puncturing the fabric and to keep the fine down clusters from working their way out through the pores of the fabric. The baffle must be breathable, to allow the down clusters to expand and provide good insulation, and the outer fabric must have a high thread count (be tightly woven) to prevent the insulation from escaping.

Foam. For items that require good resiliency, foam works well. It comes in many thicknesses and densities. For thin products, craft foam (⅛ inch thick) sandwiched between layers of fabric is fine. For upholstery-related items, foam slabs are required. Many fabric stores and home/ hardware warehouses carry these. Foam (polyurethane) is classified by its indentation load deflection (ILD; the amount of pressure needed to push the foam down) and its density: The higher the ILD, the firmer the foam; the higher the density, the longer-wearing the foam will be. Thus, a high ILD with a low density yields a stiff foam with a short life, and a low ILD with a high density yields a soft foam with a longer life. Unless you go to an industrial rubber or upholstery supplier, you may not have these choices. If you decide to make a covered foam mattress, I recommend that you talk with a local upholsterer, feel samples of various foams, and have them order you a piece cut to size. It is well worth the expense.

That's it for tools and techniques! A few, simple, readily available materials and some key tools are all you need to sew practically anything you can imagine for the kitchen, bath, garden, shop, or travel.

OTHER FILLINGS

For some applications, odd fillings are needed. Here are some of the ones I have used:

- **Saw dust or wood shavings**. For firm stuffing, aromatic wood scraps work well. To protect against moths in a storage closet, you can use cedar shavings inside a door jamb or to pad a pillow.

- **Clay cat litter**. Clay is heavy and absorbs odors. This can be a desirable filling for a fabric-covered weight (used to weight pattern pieces on fabric while laying them out for cutting), or for a scented item, such as a draft dodger used to fill the crack under a door. Essential oils can be used to scent the clay; it will hold and emit the scent for a long time.

- **Rice, beans, and beads.** Stuffed animals and other beanbag constructions can be filled with a variety of readily available, small objects. If the item might get wet, do not use foodstuffs — plastic beads, often available by the pound, are a better choice. You can make all kinds of games for kids with simple shapes and common fillings.

three

Sew Simple: Flat and Functional Items

- *Tarp*
- *Shower Curtain*
- *Harvest/Log Tote*
- *Bandana Bundle*
- *Apron*
- *Elastic Towel Wrap*

Combining **flat pieces of fabric** with various trims and findings is an easy way to make practical products. The projects in this chapter will familiarize you with the most basic sewing and finishing techniques, and the items themselves are useful and fun.

My hope is that you will gain creative freedom from using this book. Becoming comfortable in working with new materials and making your own patterns is the first step toward that goal. If you have never sewn without a store-bought pattern, these projects will help you see that circles, rectangles, and triangles trimmed in different ways can result in functional items you can be proud of.

Practice yourself, for heaven's sake, in little things; and thence proceed to greater.

— EPICTETUS, *DISCOURSES*, BOOK II, CHAPTER 5

MEASURE TWICE, CUT ONCE

As for any step-by-step task, always read instructions completely before beginning your work. It will make all the difference, particularly as the projects become more complex.

Tarp

To call this project a tarp is to limit its potential! A hemmed rectangle of cloth is as versatile as the fabric choices and sizes available to you. Make it waterproof to protect firewood outside or decorative to cover furniture at your summer cabin. Let your imagination be your guide.

An 8-foot square tarp is a good, useful size, but the chart below offers you lots of other options.

Materials

3 yards fabric (canvas, pack cloth, or other fabric suitable for outdoor use), 96" wide (4–7 yards, if narrower)

Grommets, with holes large enough to accommodate clothesline rope

Metal die or special pliers

Sewing thread

FINDING OR MAKING EXTRAWIDE FABRIC

Extrawide cloth can be difficult to find in fabric stores. It is sometimes available through boat supply catalogs or specialty fabric houses. If you are unable to find what you are looking for, you can make a piece of fabric large enough for a tarp, by piecing together two widths of fabric. Cut a 6-yard length of 36" wide fabric into two 3-yard lengths. Lay the two lengths of fabric on top of each other, right sides together, and, using a 1" seam allowance, stitch them along the length of the selvage. To "fell" the seam for added security, trim one layer of the seam allowance to 1/2". Fold the other layer over and around the shorter seam allowance, and stitch the seam allowances down at 1/8" from the edge, and again at 3/8" in from the edge. You have now created a double-needle, flat-felled seam and made a piece of fabric that is twice as wide as you had before. (See page 24 for more on felled seams.)

The math. If you want a perfectly square tarp, start with enough fabric so that when you cut it in half and double its width, it will be square (see chart). Note that 2" of the width is taken up in the 1" center seam allowance, and that 8" of both the length and the width is used to make a reinforced hem. Of course, for even larger sizes, you can triple the width (taking into account that there will be two seam allowances).

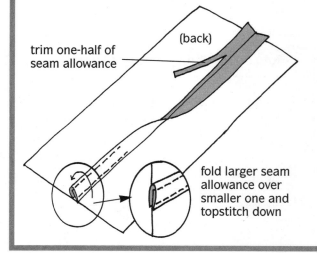

trim one-half of seam allowance

(back)

fold larger seam allowance over smaller one and topstitch down

The Math Explained

SINGLE WIDTH	DOUBLED WIDTH	LENGTH OF FABRIC NEEDED FOR SQUARE TARP	TARP SIZE
36"	70"	4 yards	62 x 62"
45"	88"	5 yards	80 x 80"
54"	106"	6 yards	98 x 98"
60"	118"	7 yards	110 x 110"

Hemming and Making Mitered Corners

1 After marking and cutting out your tarp in the desired shape (square or rectangular) and size, press under 2" twice toward the back of the fabric, on all four sides.

2 To make mitered corners that eliminate bulk, unfold the pressed seam allowances. Fold in each corner diagonally across the innermost corner point, and press. Unfold corner and trim the diagonal to 1/2" beyond the pressed edge. Fold the mitered corners in.

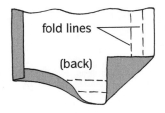

fold lines

(back)

1. FOLD CORNER IN

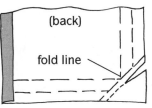

(back)

fold line

2. TRIM 1/2" FROM FOLD LINE

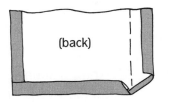

(back)

3. FOLD HEMS BACK IN

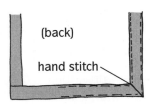

(back)

hand stitch

4. TOPSTITCH HEMS

3 Topstitch at 1/8" from the inside turned edge, and again 1/4" in from the outer tarp edge, to secure the hems down.

4 Attach grommets at each corner, and at evenly spaced intervals around the tarp. The tripled fabric along the hemmed edges should be thick enough to give you a sturdy anchor for metal grommets, and to withstand the stress of clothesline rope being pulled through the grommets.

CREATIVE FINISH: WAXING THE CANVAS

If you're using cotton fabric, you can purchase various spray or brush-on water repellent sealers (nylon is naturally water repellent). You can also make your own hand wax for canvas.

Materials

2 cups boiled linseed oil
2 ounces beeswax
2 ounces rosin

1. Heat the beeswax and rosin in a double boiler or in a 250°F oven until they are melted and combined.

2. Add the oil and stir.

3. Stretch the canvas and brush on the warm mixture, allowing it to dry between coats. Repeat this three times (you will have to reheat the mixture; each coat takes a long time to dry).

This old-fashioned coating makes a stiff tarp that should be stored hanging or rolled rather than folded; otherwise the coating could crack, particularly if it is cold.

GROMMETS EVENLY SPACED

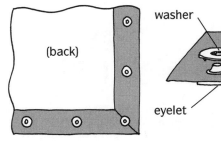

(back)

washer

eyelet

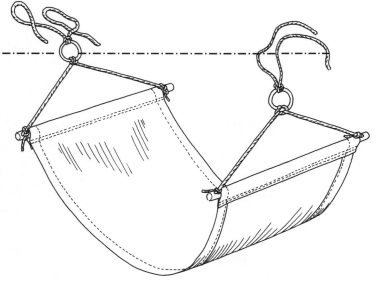

VARIATION: HAMMOCK

Make this flat hammock out of practical or decorative fabric for a lovely addition to your deck or backyard. Use coated canvas or naturally water-repellent nylon to keep the hammock dry, so you can use it all spring and summer, and even shortly after a rain shower.

Materials

90 x 36" piece heavy fabric

Two 36" long x 1½" diameter dowels

Two 6" or larger metal rings

Two 2–3 yard lengths rope (cotton rope at least ⅜" thick, nylon as small as ¼")

Heavy rope (for hanging)

Sewing thread (preferably nylon upholstery thread, for strength)

1 To make a simple hammock, hem the sides of the fabric by turning under 1" twice along both 90" edges, and topstitch close to the inside turned edge.

2 Turn and press under 1" at each end; make a 5" fold and stitch it down close to the turned under edge and again ¾" in from that.

3 Drill holes 1" in from both ends of the two dowels, and insert them into the hammock casings created by the 5" folded ends.

4 Make a **lark's head knot** over the metal ring with one of the 2- to 3-yard lengths of rope.

hold loop behind metal ring

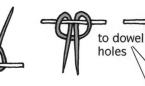

pull lower ends through loop

pull down

tighten

5 Thread each end of the rope through the holes at either end of the dowel. Loop the rope around the dowel and tie a **bowline knot.**

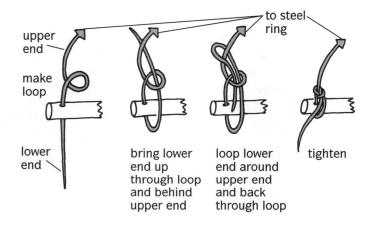

upper end

make loop

lower end

bring lower end up through loop and behind upper end

loop lower end around upper end and back through loop

to steel ring

tighten

6 Repeat steps 4 and 5 for the other dowel and knot, so that the ends won't pull back through.

7 Hang the hammock from ropes attached to the steel rings and tied to trees.

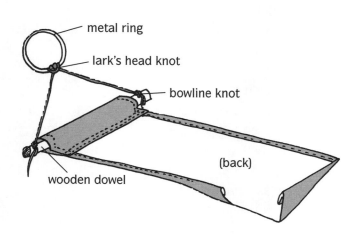

metal ring

lark's head knot

bowline knot

(back)

wooden dowel

Shower Curtain

If you're like me, at one time or another you may have searched high and low for a shower curtain to transform the look of your bathroom or, at the very least, to match new decor. Search no more! Now you can make your own shower curtain and will have the added luxury of choosing from a wide selection of fabric sizes, colors, designs, and patterns at the fabric store.

A shower curtain is like a specialized tarp that hangs vertically. You can choose a waterproof fabric to make a single-layered curtain, or you can make a second, outer curtain from more decorative fabric. Plasticized and vinyl fabrics are rather sticky to sew and can get caught on the needle plate of the sewing machine. To avoid this, sew with a sheet of tissue paper underneath the fabric and tear it out of the seam when you are finished. The following instructions can be used to make both a single-layer waterproof curtain and a decorative outer curtain. They are for a standard-sized shower curtain measuring 72 x 72".

Materials

4½ yards fabric, at least 36" wide
Large metal or plastic grommets
Metal die and hammer or special pliers
Curtain weights (1")
Sewing thread

Cutting Layout

If you have chosen fabric with a pattern that must be matched horizontally or vertically, you will need extra fabric to do so. Determine the dimensions you need, draw the pieces on the wrong side of the fabric, and cut out. The pieces in this project are:

Two curtain panels, 80 x 36" (for a 69" wide curtain); 80 x 45" (for a 87" wide curtain)

Length: The top and bottom hems will require 4" of fabric each. A length of 80" will result in a curtain 72" long.

Width: The center join seam will take up ½" of fabric from each panel; each side hem will take up 1" more from each panel. Two 36" wide panels will result in a finished curtain width of 69". To make a curtain exactly 72" wide, cut each panel 37½" wide.

Making the Curtain

1 Place the fabric panels right sides together, and, using 1/2" seam allowance, stitch along one 80" edge. For a more waterproof finish, make a felled seam (see page 24).

2 Press under 1/2" twice along both side edges of the curtain. Stitch 1/8 to 3/16" from the inside folded edge.

3 Press under 2" twice along the top edge of the curtain. Stitch 1/8 to 3/16" from the inside folded edge, and again along the top edge.

4 Press under 2" along the bottom hem edge. Hand stitch weights centered on the hem allowance, stitching through the two layers of hem. Press under the second 2" hem allowance to conceal the weights. Stitch close to the inside folded edge.

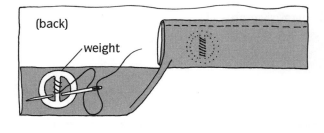

Attaching the Grommets

5 Decide how close together you want your grommets located (generally 6–10" apart). Making sure that you locate one grommet within 1" of each end, mark equidistant grommet points across the top hem of the curtain. Following the instructions given for either plastic or metal grommets, attach the grommets at each mark.

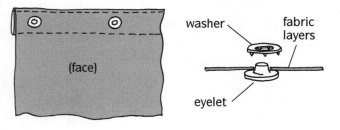

6 Use a seam sealer to waterproof all seams on the curtain liner (see Waterproofing Seams box below).

HOW MANY GROMMETS?

You can add grommets to one or more curtains and hang them together on standard shower curtain hooks, or you can make a plastic liner and a decorative outer curtain, and attach one set of grommets through both curtains for a permanently lined curtain. Consider the issue of laundering when making this decision.

WATERPROOFING SEAMS

Any hole in a waterproof fabric, regardless of the size, is a place that can potentially leak water. Therefore, seal all seams after sewing a waterproof fabric. You can purchase seam sealant from camping and industrial fabric suppliers. Apply the sealant to all seamed areas and allow to dry overnight.

Harvest/Log Tote

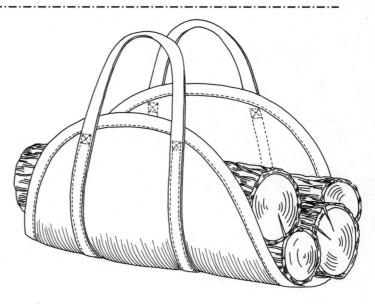

This flat, round circle of cloth is easy to make and serves a variety of practical purposes. Lay it flat on the ground as you load it up with firewood or freshly harvested greens; then grab the handles to form a sling, and carry your stash into the house. Heavy canvas is a good choice for this project, due to its weight and its inherent water-repellent properties. You may also choose to make an outer cover of vinyl or nylon, or line the tote with a waterproof fabric. Consider the issue of laundering, when making your fabric choices.

Materials

1⅛ yards heavy canvas, 36" wide (1 full yard after shrinkage)

1⅛ yard waterproof fabric (optional)

3½ yards double-fold bias binding, at least ½" wide

5 yards nylon strap webbing, 1 or 2" wide

Sewing thread

Cutting Layout

Draw a 36" diameter circle on the fabric, and cut out (see box, "How to Mark Large Circles," page 47). If you want to line the tote with a waterproof fabric, cut a 36" diameter circle out of that fabric as well.

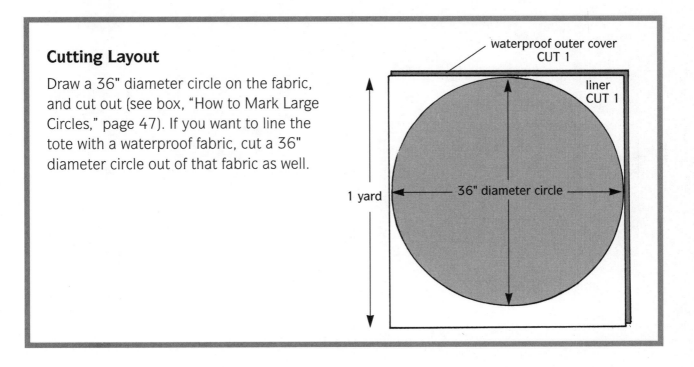

waterproof outer cover
CUT 1

liner
CUT 1

1 yard

36" diameter circle

Creating the Tote

1 Lay the waterproof fabric circle on the canvas circle, wrong sides together. Bind the entire circumference of the circle with double-fold bias binding (see page 29). Decide which surface you want to be the outside of the tote (the outside surface will touch the ground most frequently, so it should be the most water repellent).

2 On the outside of the tote mark two points on one diameter line, (drawn when making the original circle), 9" in from the outer edges. These points are where the strap will go around the bottom of the log carrier. On each end of the other diameter, locate two points 4" to either side of the line, along the circumference of the circle. These are the points where the strap will form a loop to become the handles. Draw chalk lines connecting these points.

3 Starting at one of the 9" marks, pin the strap webbing onto the outside of the tote, centered along these lines. Make 18" loops at each end for the handles. Continue pinning the webbing along the marked lines until you reach the starting point. Turn under 1" at the end of the webbing, and pin over the raw edge of the webbing at the starting point, to make a clean hem. Cut off the excess. Sew the webbing onto the tote by stitching ⅛" in from each edge.

4 Make box stitches where the webbing ends join, and at all four handle stress points.

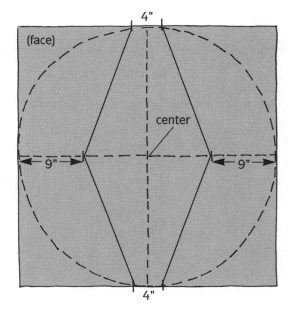

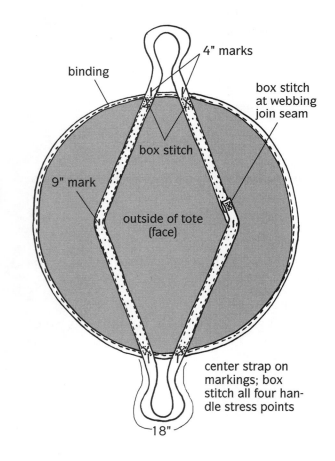

How to Mark Large Circles

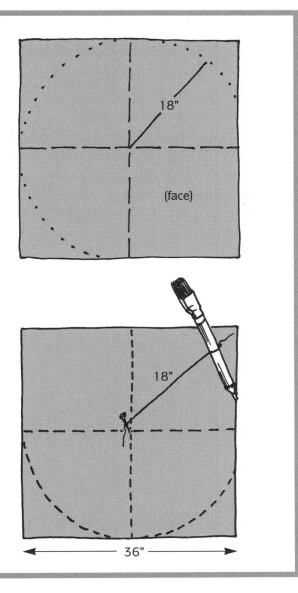

Method 1: Start by marking, with chalk, a square on the right side of the fabric. Mark the midpoint of each side, and draw two intersecting lines to find the center of the square. Measure from the center point to the edge of the square and mark the radius all the way around.

Method 2: Find the center of the square as in Method 1. Make a temporary compass by tying a pin to one end of a length of string, and a chalk pencil to the other, 18" from the pin (or whatever size you want your circle's radius to be). Place the pin at the center point, and pivot around this point to mark a circle on the right side of the fabric.

Bandana Bundle

Here's the classic "run away from home with your bag tied to the end of a fishing pole" bag. You can make this drawstring pouch without making a turned-under casing. By using two prehemmed bandanas, this bag can be made in minutes. Use two different colored bandanas to make a two-tone reversible bag.

Materials

Two 22 x 22" bandanas
2 yards cord that will fit easily through a 1" casing (e.g., string, twine, raffia, shoelace, cotton/nylon rope)
Sewing thread

Creating the Drawstring Casing

1 Iron the bandanas to remove any creases.

2 Lay one bandana on top of the other at a diagonal, wrong sides together, so that there are eight even corner points showing. Pin together.

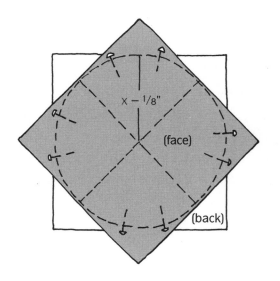

3 Find the midpoint of each side of the top bandana and mark with chalk. Draw two intersecting lines across the bandana by connecting these midpoints. The intersection of the two lines is the center point of the bandana.

4 Measure from the center point to the edge of the bandana (x), and deduct 1/8" from this length. Do the same all around the bandana to form a circle. Connect the marks to form the circular sewing line.

5 Following the instructions in step 4, mark a second circle, 1" smaller than the first, inside the first circle.

6 At two opposite points of the bandana, affix pins across these two marked circle lines, 3/4" on either side of the center point (these will be the two places where the drawstring exits the casing).

7 Starting at one of the pins, stitch around the outer circle to the next pin, backstitching several times at the start and end of the seam. Leave a 1 1/2" opening between the two pins, and stitch from the second pin around the outer circle to the next pin, again leaving a 1 1/2" opening between the two pins, and backstitching at both ends.

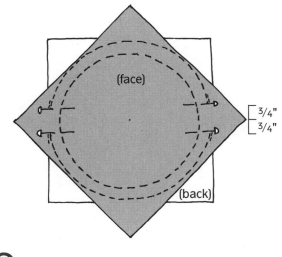

8 Stitch all the way around the inner circle.

Assembling the Pouch

9 Cut two 36" pieces of cord. Attach a safety pin to one end of the cord. Starting at one of the openings, thread the pinned end of the cord through and all the way around the casing. Tie the two ends of the cord together. Starting at the opposite opening, thread the other 36" cord through the casing in the same way, and tie the two ends together with a knot.

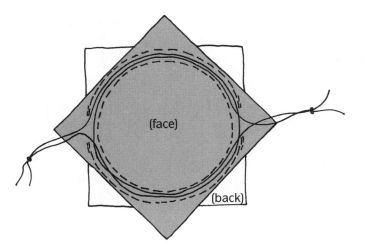

10 Adjust the fabric so the gathers are evenly distributed around the circle; adjust the cords so the knots become the pulling ends. Push in the center of the bag to form a pouch. Pull both cords at the same time to close the bag securely.

VARIATION: FABRIC REMNANT BUNDLE

You can make a similar bag out of fabric remnants instead of bandanas, but this time you need to finish the edges by lining the fabric. Use light-weight fabric — heavy fabric will make the drawstring casing too thick for the cord to pull it closed.

Materials
Four 23 x 23" pieces light-weight fabric
2 yards cord (to fit through a 1" casing)
Sewing thread

1 Draw and cut out four 23" squares of one or more different fabrics.

2 With right sides together and using a 1/2" seam allowance, stitch around the outer edge of two fabric pieces, leaving a 3" opening on one side.

3 Turn right-side out, press, and then stitch 1/8" in from the edge around the entire square to finish.

4 Follow steps 1–3 for the other two pieces of fabric.

5 Using the two doubled pieces of fabric instead of bandanas, complete the drawstring pouch following steps 2–10 in the main project instructions.

Apron

Aprons are used for many different things; choose your fabric depending on the function of the apron. Light-weight printed fabric is great for kitchen aprons; for really messy uses, consider using a waterproof fabric. Canvas makes a terrific base for painted, stenciled, or printed embellishments. You can decorate the fabric pieces before or after marking and cutting, or after the apron is assembled.

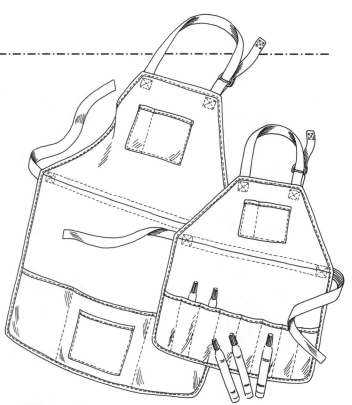

Materials

1 yard fabric, at least 36" wide

2 yards cotton webbing, twill tape, or grosgrain ribbon, 1" wide (for straps); or nylon strapping

4 yards double-fold bias binding, ½" wide

Two 1" metal D rings

Sewing thread

Cutting Layout

Following the measurements and layout shown, draw the pieces on the wrong side of the fabric, mark and cut out.

The pieces in this project are:

A. Apron bottom, 18 x 18", with rounded bottom corners

B. Apron bib, 8" wide at top, 18" wide at bottom, 12" long

C. Pockets, 6 x 6"

D. Tool pocket, 18" wide x 8" long, with rounded bottom corners

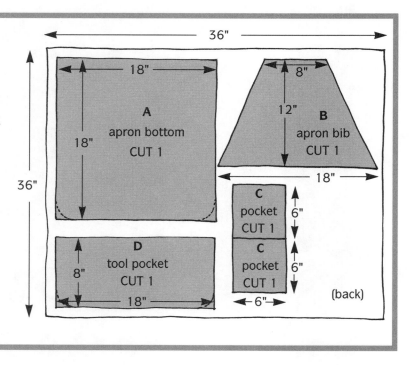

Attaching the Pockets

1 Attach the bias binding to the top edges of the three pocket pieces (see page 29).

2 Turn under and press ½" on the side edges of the two 6" pockets.

3 Pin one 6" pocket so that it is 8" down from the top edge of the bib, upside down, with right sides together. Stitch the pocket bottom to the bib. Flip the pocket up, and sew the sides to the bib, ⅛" in from the pocket edges, backstitching at the pocket corners several times. Stitch a seam 2" in from one edge, to make the slot for holding pens.

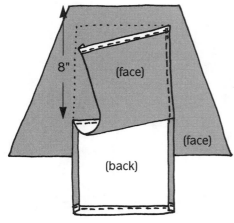

4 Pin the bottom edge of the other 6" pocket in the center of the larger tool pocket, 1½" up from the bottom edge, upside down, with right sides together. Using a ½" seam allowance, stitch along the bottom edge. Flip the pocket up, and sew the sides to the larger pocket, stitching ⅛" from the pocket edges, backstitching several times at the pocket corners.

5 Pin the large pocket to the apron bottom, right side of the apron facing the wrong side of the pocket, matching the side and bottom edges. Stitch two vertical lines 6" in from each side edge, to form the center 6" pocket.

6 Using a ¼" seam allowance, stitch around the outer edge of the large pocket.

Putting It All Together

7 Using a ½" seam allowance, stitch the bib to the apron, right sides together. Press the seam open.

8 Bind around the entire apron body (see page 29), catching the raw edges of the tool pocket as you sew around the lower half. Start and end the binding at an upper bib corner, so the binding join will be concealed underneath a strap.

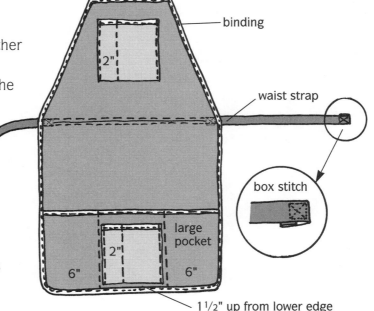

Attaching the Straps

9 Cut one 20" length, one 3" length, and one 48" length of strap material.

10 Find the center point of the 48" strap and the center point of the bib join seam (back side). Pin these points together. (For a 48" waist strap, 15" will extend out on either side of the apron.) Pin the rest of the strapping to the apron, evenly covering the bib join seam. Stitch the strapping ⅛" in on either side of the strap-to-apron join seam. Box stitch at both ends of the waist strap over the bias binding. Turn under 1" twice and hem the raw ends of the waist tie straps using box stitches. (If using nylon strapping, singe ends over a candle to heat seal rather than hemming.)

11 Fold under 1" on the 20" length of strapping, and with the raw edge of the strapping facing the apron fabric, stitch it to the front left-hand bib corner, making a box stitch to hold the strap on securely. Turn under ½", then 1", on the raw end of the strap, and make a box stitch to hem it.

12 Fold under 1" of the 3" length of strapping, and pin it to the right-hand corner of the bib. Thread the **D** rings through the 1" piece of strapping, and tuck the end under the 1" fold, so it will be caught in the back of the box stitch. Box stitch through all three layers of strapping to secure the **D** rings to the apron.

13 Thread the longer length of neck strap through both **D** rings, and then back out through one **D** ring to hold it in place.

14 When taking off the apron, loosen the neck strap, leaving it secured to the **D** rings, then lift the neckstrap over your head. Tighten the neck strap comfortably when you put the apron back on. You also might consider using snap buckles instead of **D** rings to secure the neck strap.

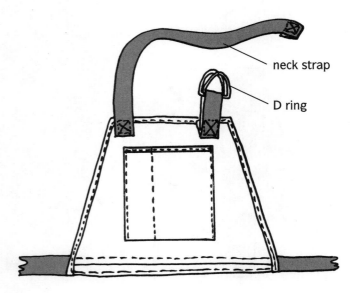

neck strap

D ring

DESIGN OPTIONS

✂ **Pleated or billowed pockets.** Make more complex three-dimensional pockets by using the pattern for the Bucket Caddy (see page 103), or design your own, by cutting the tool pocket so that the top is slightly wider than the bottom. Stitch around the sides and bottom, and then bind to finish the edges, carefully arranging the excess fabric to make slightly billowed pockets.

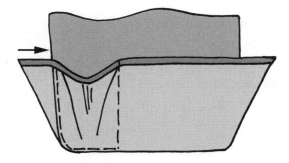

✂ **Children's art apron.** Scale down the size of the apron patterns to fit a child. Measure the child's waist, and the length from the neck to waist, and waist to knees. Use these measurements to resize the apron bib and bottom, and adjust the pockets accordingly. Stitch many vertical lines in the larger pocket, (you can also make several layers of these pockets as in the Traveling Jewelry Bag's earring pockets, page 111), to make dividers just the right size for crayons or felt tip markers.

✂ **Different findings.** For variety, use D rings, buckles, ties, or hook and loop fasteners for the strap, neck, and waist closures.

DECORATING OPTIONS

You can decorate the apron with fabric paints either before or after you sew it. Each type of fabric paint comes with specific instructions on how to permanently "fix" the paint so it lasts though repeated launderings. Custom decorating is a wonderful way to personalize sewn gifts. Add vegetable and flower motifs for the gardener, or a palette with bright-colored paint blotches for the artist. Drawings of herbs, utensil designs, and key words from recipes make a special apron for the cook.

There are many different ways to decorate fabric:

✂ Fine-line squeeze bottles of fabric paints are great for detailed decorations and words.

✂ Sponges and brushes allow you to create larger designs.

✂ Stenciling lends itself to fabric embellishment. You can purchase stencils, or, for an even more personal touch, make your own using a box knife or X-ACTO knife and cardboard or mylar sheets. Use a sponge or stiff brush to dab or push thick fabric paint or stencil creme paints into the stencil. Add details with a brush or squeeze bottle once the stencil is dry.

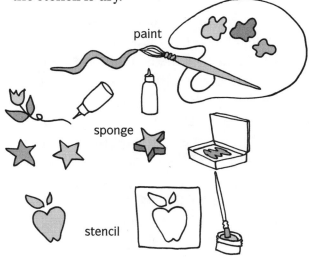

paint

sponge

stencil

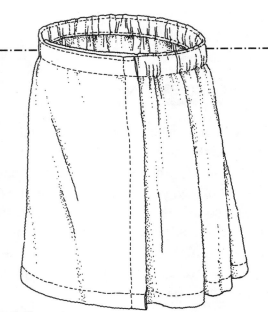

Elastic Towel Wrap

Using terry cloth is great fun, and people love gifts made out of terry cloth because it is a practical and cozy fabric. Be sure to launder your piece of fabric in hot water and dry on a hot setting to make it shrink as much as possible before you sew. The elastic and hook and loop fastener allow you to make a towel wrap that fits most everyone with one additional benefit: It stays in place!

Materials

1½ yards preshrunk cotton terry cloth,
   or a large towel
24" of elastic, nonroll type, 2" wide
10" hook and loop fastener, 2" wide
Large safety pin
Sewing thread

Cutting Layout

The length and width of the towel wrap pattern are based on two factors: (1) Will this be made to fit a man's waist or a woman's bust? Measure the waist or bust, and add 12" to this measurement. (For example, for a 34" girth, make it 46" long.) (Note: 6" of waist or bust adjustment [ease] is built into the pattern — the hook and loop closure allows you to fasten it wherever it feels comfortable.) Although this is the width of the garment, it is the longer of the two measurements, and will, therefore, run the length of the fabric; and (2) How long do you want the towel to hang? Decide on the length, and add 6" to this measurement (which will run the width of the fabric). (For example, for a 30" length, make it 36" long.)

After determining the size of the pattern, draw on the wrong side of the fabric and cut out, making one of the long edges (width measurement) run along, and include, the selvage (this will help eliminate bulk in the elastic casing). You can also use a finished towel, to eliminate the need to hem the bottom and sides.

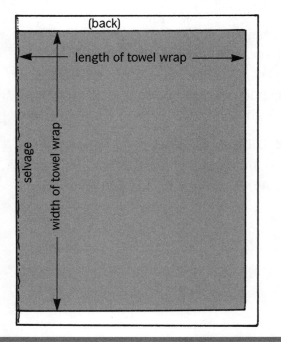

Hemming the Sides and Bottom

1 On both sides of the rectangular fabric piece, turn under and press 1" twice, toward the wrong side of the fabric. Topstitch ⅛" from both edges to hem.

2 On the bottom of the wrap (the non-selvage side), turn under and press 1", then 2", toward the wrong side of the fabric, to form the bottom hem. Stitch ⅛" from the inside edge, and again, ¼" from the edge of the hem bottom. *(Note: Instead of hemming, you can bind the side and bottom edges with bias binding, if desired.)*

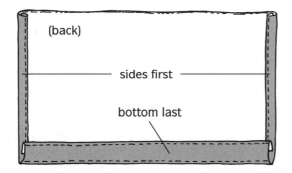

(back)

— sides first —

bottom last

Making the Elastic Casing

3 On the top edge of the wrap (selvage side), turn under and press 3". Open the pressed edge.

4 Measure in 10" in from each side, and mark with a pin. Gently stretch a piece of elastic between the two pins, and cut this length (which shound be about ⅔ the full distance between the pins, depending on the resiliency of your elastic). Pin one end of the elastic at the left-hand 10" mark, (pin perpendicular to top edge of wrap), ½" down from the casing fold. Pin a large safety pin to the other end of the elastic. Fold the pressed casing back down, and stitch across the width

of the casing along the left-hand edge of the elastic, through all layers, to attach the elastic where it is pinned.

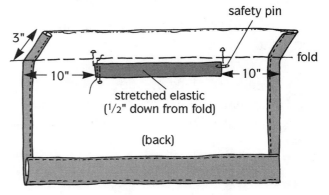

safety pin

3"

fold

10"   10"

stretched elastic
(½" down from fold)

(back)

5 With the casing lying flat, pin the elastic in a few spots to hold it in place. Stitch down the casing, ¼" from the edge of the selvage, from the left-hand hemmed edge to the right-hand 10" pin mark, being careful not to catch the elastic in the seam. Remove all straight pins from the elastic. Grab the safety pin (through the fabric), and pull the elastic to the right-hand pin mark. Pin, then stitch across the width of the casing to anchor the elastic at this point. The towel will now have gathers where it is elasticized.

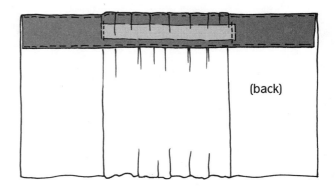

(back)

6 Finish stitching the casing to the other side.

7 Topstitch the casing ¼" from the top edge, being careful not to catch the elastic.

Attaching the Hook and Loop

8 Place the 10" piece of hook ¼" in from one end of the wrap, centered on the inside (back) of the casing. Stitch around all edges to secure.

9 Place a 10" piece of loop ¼" in from the other end of the wrap, centered on the outside (front) of the casing. Stitch around all edges to secure.

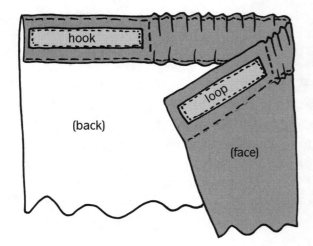

DECORATING OPTIONS

✂ The towel wrap can be decorated with a variety of trims, which can easily be stitched on along the hem or casing seams. Trims designed for curtains and drapes, like pom-poms and fringe, can add playfulness to the terry cloth wrap, particularly if it is to be used at the pool or beach.

✂ If you are a needleworker, consider embroidered or appliquéd borders around the wrap.

✂ Pockets can also be added. If embellished before stitching them to the wrap, they provide both function and decoration.

four
Practical Pockets: Custom Containers

- Seed Packet Roll
- Rigid Paintbrush Portfolio
- Tool Roll
- Sun Visor Organizer
- Passport Pouch

Now that we have covered some basic flat shapes, we can begin to make more complex items by adding layers of fabric. Pockets are nothing more than clean-finished second layers of fabric, open at one end to hold items. They are simple and can lead to an infinite variety of form and function in your designs.

The pockets outlined in this chapter are basic, flat pockets, varied in shape, size, and their intended end use. Knowing how and having the confidence to make pockets is essential in working toward personalized designs. It is a wonderful feeling to be able to make a one-of-a-kind organizer that perfectly holds its contents as you had planned!

The projects in this chapter are suggestions — jumping-off points for creating your own useful items. Once you learn the basics, you can experiment with different fabrics, shapes, and accessories (such as zippers, bias binding, and findings).

Seed Packet Roll

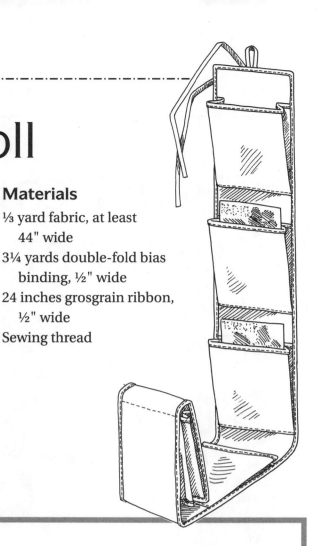

Hanging storage is easy to make and to customize. This design, sized to fit standard (3½ x 5¼") garden seed packets, makes a nice gift for gardening enthusiasts. Since seed packets aren't very heavy, any stable woven fabric will do. Try calico or plain-weave mid-weight cotton. For a more durable pouch, use a twill weave. If you don't plan to decorate the fabric yourself, garden print motifs add a nice touch. You might also consider using clear vinyl for the pockets, so that the packets themselves become the colorful decoration.

Materials

⅓ yard fabric, at least
  44" wide
3¼ yards double-fold bias
  binding, ½" wide
24 inches grosgrain ribbon,
  ½" wide
Sewing thread

Cutting Layout

Fold the fabric in half, selvage to selvage, right sides together. Following the measurements and layout shown, draw the pieces on the wrong side of the fabric, mark, and cut out.

The pieces in this project are:

A. Backing, 4" wide x 40" long, (cut on the fold)

B. Pockets, 6" wide x 5½" long

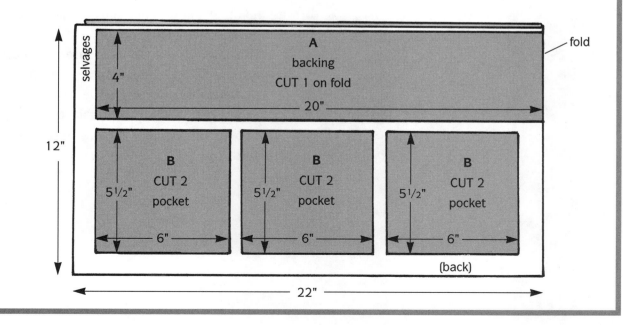

Preparing the Pockets

1 On the back of each pocket, mark the pleat lines 3/4" and 1 1/4" in from both 5 1/2" edges.

2 Bind the top 6" edge of each pocket (see page 29).

3 Stitch along the four marked lines on each pocket, stitching straight over the binding.

4 Fold the pleat lines to form a large box pleat (see page 26) and press in.

5 On the bottom of the pockets, turn under and press 1/2" toward the wrong side of the fabric to form the bottom hems. Hand baste in place.

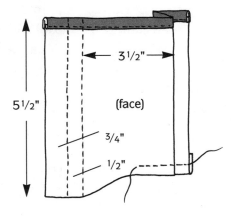

Backing the Pockets

6 Pin the wrong sides of the pockets to the right side of the backing so that the pleat extensions line up with the edge of the backing. Pin the first pocket 2" from the top of the backing. Pin the remaining five pockets below the first, leaving 1 1/2" in between each. The bottom pocket should be 1/2" up from the bottom of the backing. Use several pins to keep the pockets well aligned and evenly spaced.

7 Stitch along the sides of the backing 1/4" from the edge, catching the edges of all the pockets. Do not catch the pleats in the stitching.

8 Topstitch 1/8" from the turned edge, across the bottom of each pocket. For a decorative effect, you might choose to stitch ribbon or bric-a-brac trim along the pocket bottoms, adjoining the raw edges of the trim with the edges of the backing.

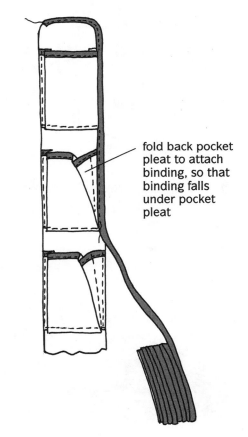

fold back pocket pleat to attach binding, so that binding falls under pocket pleat

Binding and Finishing

9 Round all four corners of the backing, and fold back and pin all pocket pleats away from the edges. Bind the periphery of the seed packet roll (see page 29).

10 Turn under 1/2" twice on both ends of the ribbon, and stitch these hems.

11 Fold the ribbon in half and stitch to the top of the binding, on the back of the hanging roll, so that a 2" loop extends above the top. This forms the hanging loop and the ties.

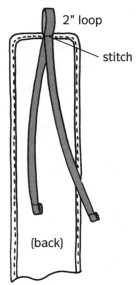

2" loop

stitch

(back)

12 *To hang,* simply loop the ribbon over a hook or nail. *To roll,* start at the bottom, folding each pocket over the next. When you reach the top, tie the ribbon around the whole bundle of seed packets.

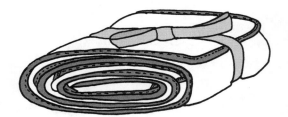

DECORATING OPTIONS

The pockets in this project are like little blank canvases waiting to be decorated. Before you sew, mark the seam allowances and pleat lines on the fabric, to delinate the 3½ x 5" face of each pocket.

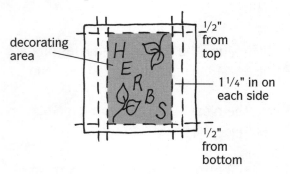

decorating area

½" from top

1¼" in on each side

½" from bottom

✂ Decide how you want to categorize your seeds. Using fabric paints, mark labels on the pockets, for example, "Herbs," "Greens," "Flowers," or "Beans and Peas." "Cool Weather Starts" and "Warm Weather Starts" is another way to classify seeds. You can also paint leaves and flowers on the pockets.

✂ Embroider the pockets with a variety of designs.

✂ Use an alphabet stencil set to do lettering, or make a border around the edge of each pocket.

✂ If giving this as a gift, fill the hanging roll full of seeds. You might want to fill the bottom pocket with blank plant markers and a permanent marking pen, to label seed starts.

✂ Craft stores carry all sorts of plastic, ceramic and papier-mâché shapes and trinkets — such as miniature carrots, flower pots, and garden tools — that you can hang like fringe from the corners of each pocket.

Rigid Paintbrush Portfolio

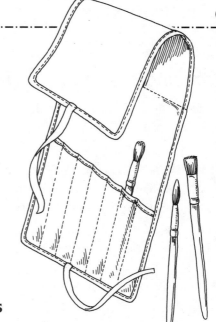

This pattern is for a rigid portfolio that will not bend. It can be modified to create all kinds of portfolios. Turn the entire design 90 degrees so that the "hinge" is on the side, and make a portfolio to hold important papers or a calendar. You can use this easy, versatile technique to make desk accessories, sewing kits, and notebook covers that are custom-fit for your needs and express your creativity!

Materials

⅔ yard of fabric, 36" wide (canvas, twill, or pack cloth)
3 yards of double-fold bias binding, ½" wide
9 x 12" piece cardboard
24" grosgrain ribbon, ½" wide; or nylon ribbon

Cutting Layout

Starting with a single layer of fabric, fold in one selvage 10", in order to cut two of pattern piece A from the folded goods. Following the measurements as shown, draw the pieces on fabric and cut out.

The pieces in this project are:

A1 and **A2.** Portfolio inner and outer covers, 10" wide x 24" long, with rounded corners

B. Inner brush pocket, 10" wide, 10" long on one side, 7" long on the other, with rounded bottom corners

C. Cardboard, 9" wide x 12" long, with rounded bottom corners

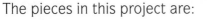
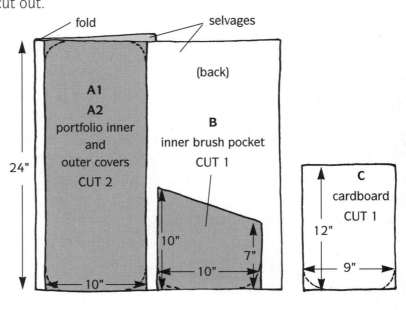

Attaching the Brush Pocket

1 Bind the top (diagonal) edge of the inner brush pocket (see page 29).

2 Pin the wrong side of the inner brush pocket to the right side of the portfolio inner cover, lining up lower and side edges. Using a 1/4" seam allowance, stitch along the bottom and sides of the pocket.

3 In chalk, mark the dividers for the brushes on the fact of the pocket. The width of these dividers will depend on the type of brushes you use. Stitch along these lines, backstitching at the top edge, over the bias binding.

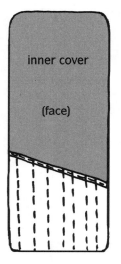

Making the Portfolio Rigid

4 Using 1/4" seam allowance, stitch together the inner and outer covers, wrong sides facing. Before stitching the top closed, insert the cardboard, and push it all the way down into the sleeve, to make the lower half rigid.

5 Topstitch across the portfolio, just above the cardboard (at the 12" mark) to hold it in place and create a fold for the top flap.

6 Center the cardboard (it should be 1/2" in from all edges), and bind the periphery of the portfolio (see page 29).

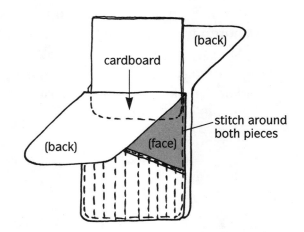

Making the Tie Closure

7 Cut two 12" pieces of ribbon. Turn under and hem one end of each piece. (If you are using nylon ribbon, you can heat seal the ends by carefully melting them over a candle.)

8 On the outside of the top flap, place the raw edge of one ribbon tie over the binding, centered, with its length running down the outer cover. Stitch along the original binding seam. Now fold the ribbon tie back over itself, so it is facing up (away from the flap), and restitch over the same seam.

9 Place the other tie on the inside bottom flap of the portfolio, over the binding, and centered on the bottom edge of the brush pocket. Attach as outlined in step 8.

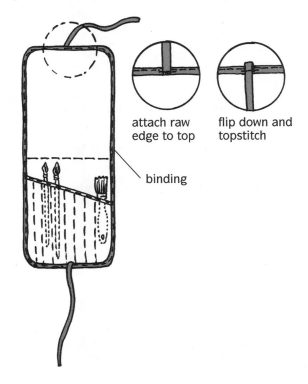

attach raw
edge to top

flip down and
topstitch

binding

VARIATION:
COSMETICS BRUSH CASE

You can make a smaller portfolio to carry makeup, using a beautiful piece of brocade for the outer cover. Choose a practical fabric that will withstand water and makeup stains for the inside layers — vinyl laminate or nylon pack cloth would work well. An extra inside pocket that can hold a mirror replaces the inserted cardboard.

Materials
8 x 18" piece of fabric
48" double-fold bias binding, ½" wide
12" ribbon or twill tape

Follow the cutting layout instructions in the main project text, making the following adjustments in pattern piece sizes:

A1 and **A2**. Portfolio inner and outer covers, 6" wide x 8" long
B. Divided cosmetics pocket, 6" wide x 2½ long
C. Mirror pocket, 6" wide x 3½" long

1 Bind the upper edges of the divided cosmetics pocket and the mirror pocket (see page 29).

2 Place the wrong side of the inner divided pocket against the right side of this mirror pocket and, using a ½" seam allowance, stitch along the bottom and sides.

3 Mark and stitch the dividing lines to create specially sized spaces for eye and lip pencils, rouge brushes, various applicators, lipsticks, and mascaras.

4 Complete the makeup portfolio following steps 4–9 (minus the cardboard insert) in the main project instructions.

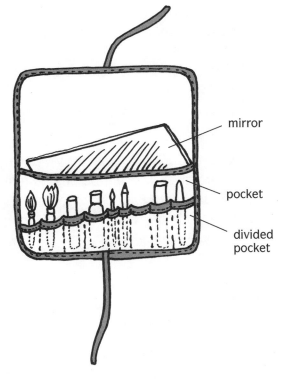

mirror

pocket

divided
pocket

Tool Roll

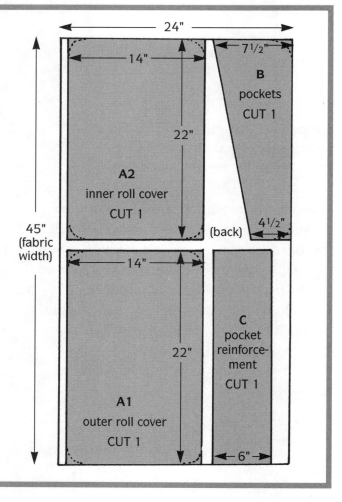

The fabric roll design described in this project can be adapted for specific tools such as chisels, screwdrivers, wrenches, brushes, picnic silverware, or any long items that need protection during transport. I've made tool rolls out of denim and leather for my many carpenter friends, and I love to see them all weathered and stained from *really* being used. By simply changing the dimensions of the slot pockets, you can personalize a gift for yourself or a friend. Use a decorative fabric on the outside and a more practical inner pocket fabric to add texture, color, and personality to the piece.

Materials

⅔ yard of canvas, at least 45" wide (1 full yard, if narrower)
4 yards double-fold bias binding, ½" wide
Hook and loop: 36" loop, 12" hook
12" twill tape or strap webbing, 1" wide
Sewing thread

Cutting Layout

Following the measurements and layout shown, draw the pieces on the fabric and cut out.

The pieces in this project are:

A1 and **A2.** Outer roll cover and inner roll cover, 22" wide x 14" long

B. Pocket, 22" wide, 4½" long on one side, 7½" long on the other

C. Reinforcement liner, 22" wide x 6" long

If your tool roll will be used for very sharp chisels or knives, it might be best to make the reinforcement liner out of leather. In this case, cut piece **C** 22" wide x 5" long and do not hem (in step 4).

Making the Hook and Loop Wraps

1 Cut two 18" pieces of loop. Cut two 6" pieces of hook. Stitch one piece of hook to the back of one loop piece, wrong sides together, leaving a 12" end with no hook backing. Repeat for the remaining hook and loop pieces.

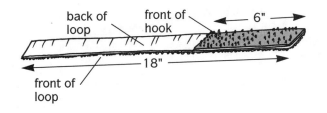

back of loop

front of hook

6"

front of loop

18"

2 On the face side of the outer roll cover, pin the unbacked end of one of the hook and loop strips to one of the 14" edges, 3½" from the bottom edge as shown, hook side down, with the hook and loop extending 5" beyond the edge of the roll. Place the second hook and loop strip 6" down from the top edge of the roll, hook side down. Starting 1" from the edge of the roll, stitch the loop strips in place, stitching around all sides of the loop.

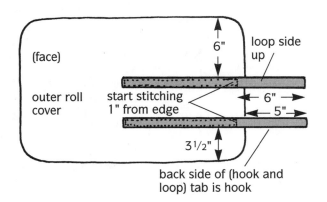

(face)

6"

loop side up

outer roll cover

start stitching 1" from edge

6"

5"

3½"

back side of (hook and loop) tab is hook

Trimming and Reinforcing the Pocket

3 Bind the top (diagonal) edge of the pocket (see page 29).

4 Press ½" toward the fabric back on both 22" edges of the reinforcement liner (if you cut this piece out of leather, omit this step).

5 With the chalk, draw a line on the face side of the inner roll cover, 3" from the bottom edge. Place one of the 22" edges of the reinforcement liner along this line, wrong side down, and, using ⅛" seam allowance, topstitch ⅛" from the top edge of the liner.

6 Draw a line on the back of the pocket, 3" up from the bottom edge. Place the pocket below the roll, face down, and lay the reinforcement liner on top of it, along this line. Topstitch ⅛" from the edge.

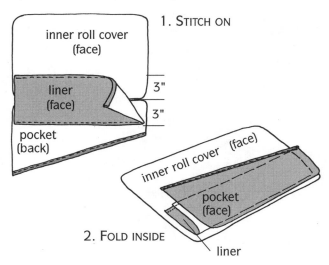

1. STITCH ON

inner roll cover (face)

liner (face)

3"

3"

pocket (back)

inner roll cover (face)

pocket (face)

2. FOLD INSIDE

liner

7 Flip the pocket up over the roll, with the liner folded perfectly in half and sandwiched in between. Line up the bottom and side edges, and topstitch around the pocket, ⅛" from the edge.

Pocket Dividers and Finishing

8 Mark the pocket dividing lines in chalk on the face of the pocket, and stitch along these lines from the bottom up, through all layers. Be careful not to catch the hook and loop strips in the dividing seams.

9 Pin and stitch the outer roll cover to the inner roll cover, wrong sides together. Trim the outer edges of the roll so that the raw seam allowance is ¼". Bind the periphery of the tool roll (see page 29).

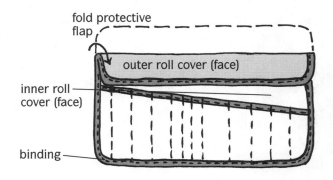

fold protective flap

outer roll cover (face)

inner roll cover (face)

binding

10 Make the handle out of a 12" strip of twill tape or strap webbing. Turn under ½" on each end, and then box stitch the turned under ends to the handle, to make 1" loops at each end.

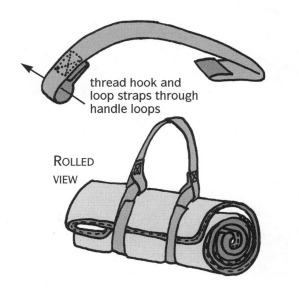

thread hook and loop straps through handle loops

ROLLED VIEW

11 *To use,* fill the tool roll with tools, fold down the protective flap, and roll up, starting at the end without the hook and loop strips. Keep the free-hanging hook and loop strips outside of the roll. When the roll is closed, thread the hook and loop strips through the handle loops, and secure.

PLANNING THE POCKET DIVIDERS

For my tool roll, I made the two end pockets 3" in from the edges, and the other eight pockets (ten total) 1½" wide.

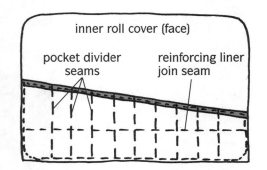

inner roll cover (face)

pocket divider seams

reinforcing liner join seam

To customize your roll before beginning to cut fabric, measure the tools you intend to store, in girth (around the handles) and length. Are there long blades to conceal fully? You may need to make the roll and pocket wider to accommodate tools with longer handles. You might also want to make the pocket straight instead of angled. The basic project construction remains the same, but all of the dimensions may require adjustment.

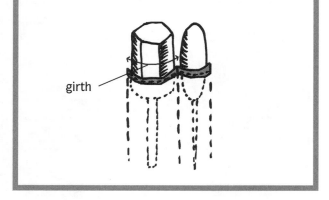

girth

DESIGN OPTIONS

✂ Modify the pattern to create a double roll. (Make sure the roll is long enough to accommodate the tool handles after it is folded in half. You may need twice as much fabric or more.)

✂ Make a tiny tool roll for yarn, tapestry, or upholstery needles.

✂ Keep all of your tent stakes in a tool roll, and you'll never lose them again!

✂ For a more decorative roll (for picnic silverware or a more whimsical tool carrier), cut two of piece A — one in a practical fabric and one in a print fabric — and baste them together, wrong sides facing. Use the plain fabric for the inner cover, and the print for the outer cover of the tool roll. The bias binding will connect the pocket and inner and outer covers of fabric.

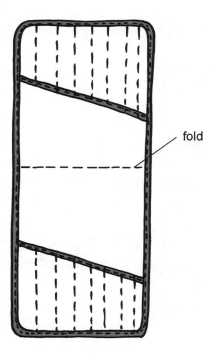

fold

Sun Visor Organizer

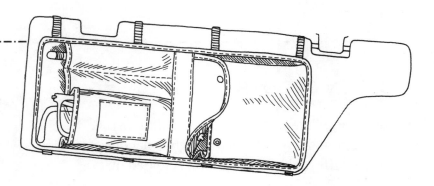

This organizer hugs your car's sun visor with elastic straps. It has a flap pocket for papers; slots for pens, tire gauges, and the like; a pocket for sunglasses; and a clear slot for a mirror. Use a durable fabric that can withstand sunlight. For this project, you will have to customize the measurements to fit your car's visor.

Materials

⅜ yard sturdy fabric, 36" wide (upholstery, vinyl, or any durable fabric that can withstand sunlight; wool and silk not recommended)

2 yards double-fold bias binding, ¼" wide

8–12" grosgrain ribbon, 1" wide

Two medium- to heavy-duty snaps

Metal die or special pliers

2½ x 3½" piece clear vinyl

1 yard elastic, ½" wide

Sewing thread

Cutting Layout

Following the measurements and layout shown, draw the pieces on the fabric and cut out.

The pieces in this project are:

A. Backing, 7½" wide x 11" long, with rounded corners

B. Pleated flap pocket, 9½" wide x 4½" long

C. Sunglasses, pen, and tire gauge pocket, 9½" wide x 5" long

D. Flap for pocket **B**, 6" wide x 2" long

E. Rectangle of clear vinyl, for front of the sunglass section of piece **C**, 2½" wide x 3½" long (not shown)

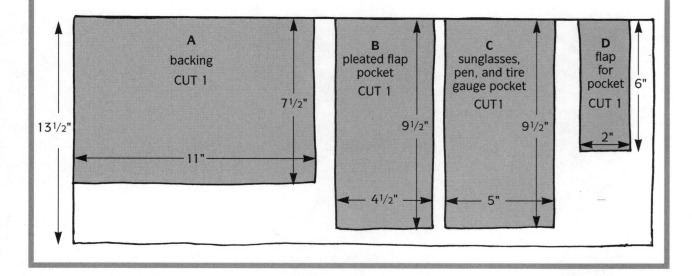

Binding

1 Bind along one long edge of the pleated flap pocket and the sunglasses, pen, and tire gauge pocket (see page 29).

2 Bind around three sides of the pocket flap, leaving one 6" side unbound.

Marking and Training the Pleats

3 On the pleated flap pocket, mark pleat lines 1" in from both sides, and again 1/2" in from those lines. Stitch along these lines, sewing up through the binding, and backstitching at the top of the binding.

4 On the sunglasses, pen, and tire gauge pocket, mark pleat lines at 1", 1 1/2", 4 1/2", and 5" from one side. Stitch along these lines, sewing up through the binding, and backstitching at the top of the binding. Using a 1/8" seam allowance, topstitch three sides of the clear vinyl rectangle onto the pocket face (to hold a mirror, if desired), with the opening toward the pocket binding.

CUSTOMIZING THE ORGANIZER

You can make the organizer as indicated in these instructions (design is based on a visor for a subcompact car), or you can measure your sun visor, and customize it to fit perfectly. Place a piece of heavy paper behind your sun visor, and trace around it, marking where the hardware and clips fasten it to the car. These obstructions determine the size and shape of the organizer.

For the length, measure the visor surface, top to bottom (**a**). For the width, measure between the clips and other obstructions, side to side (**b**). Think about where four evenly spaced verticals of elastic will fit around the visor and where they will be obstructed, and adjust accordingly. You may be able to add some width to the organizer by making it wider at the bottom, and tapering it at the top, to fit between the clips and hardware. The pocket sizes are based on the size and shape of the backing.

Once you have determined measurements (**a**) and (**b**), draw and cut out the pieces, following these formulas:

- Make piece **A**, the backing, measure (**a**) x (**b**).
- Make piece **B**, the pleated flap pocket, measure 2" longer than (**a**), and 1" narrower than half of (**b**).
- Make piece **C**, the sunglasses, pen, and tire gauge pocket, measure 2" longer than (**a**) and 1/2" narrower than half of (**b**).
- Make piece **D**, the flap for pocket B, measure 2" long x 1" narrower than (**b**).
- Make piece, **E**, the clear vinyl rectangle, measure 2 1/2 x 3 1/2".

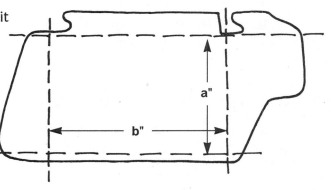

5 Press the stitched pleat lines, to train the pleats. The ½" channels should be folded to the back of the pockets, and the pleat extensions folded back toward the front, to form the pouch. Pin the pleats in place.

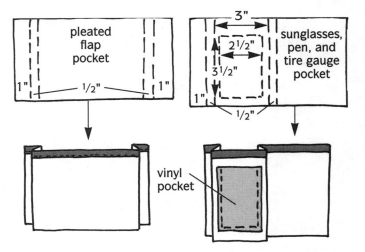

Attaching the Snaps

6 On the pleated flap pocket, mark two points 1" from the top edge, and at least 1" in from the pleat folds. Make sure they are evenly spaced. Attach the socket and ring prong parts of the snaps (see page 32).

7 Lay the flap on top of the pocket, so that it extends ¾" above the pocket. Locate the pocket snaps through the flap, and mark these two points. Attach the cap prong and stud parts of the snaps to the flap at these marks. Snap the flap to the pocket (stud on flap plugs into socket on pocket), and leave them fastened for the remainder of the project.

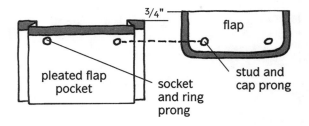

Putting It All Together

8 Pin the pockets to the backing, so that the pleat extensions of both pockets meet the edges of the backing. The pleated pocket is placed along the right-hand side of the backing, matching edges, and opens toward the center of the organizer. Stitch the tire gauge and pen divider lines at ¾" intervals from the pocket-pleat edge, across toward the outer edge. The bottom of the sunglasses, pen, and tire gauge pocket is placed so that it butts up against the top edge of the pocket flap. Trim the edges flush, and round all corners to make binding easier. Stitch ¼" from the edge, around the entire organizer.

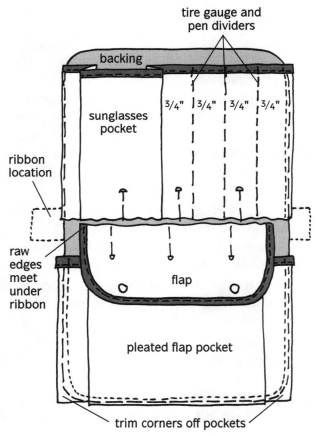

9 Pin the grosgrain ribbon down the center of the piece, covering the raw edges of the bottom of the sunglasses, pen, and tire gauge pocket, and the top of the pleated flap pocket. Stitch around the ribbon, close to the edge, to conceal these raw edges. You may want to do some decorative stitching here, such as diagonals or stripes, to add interest and hold it together more securely.

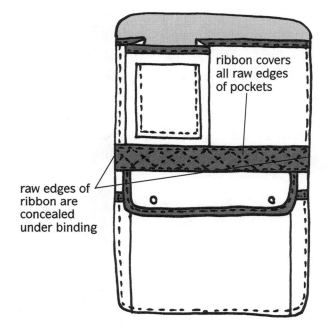

ribbon covers all raw edges of pockets

raw edges of ribbon are concealed under binding

10 Turn the organizer over, and mark four equidistant points across the top, for the four elastic loops. Make sure that these points will not interfere with any of your car's visor or hinges fasteners. Mark four points across the bottom, directly across from those at the top. At the first point, lay a piece of elastic across the backing, and stretch it gently (so it will fit snugly when secured to your car visor) to reach the corresponding point across the organizer. Cut the piece of elastic to this *stretched* length. Repeat the above procedure for the other three points on the organizer. Pin the four pieces of elastic to their respective points along the top of the backing.

11 Starting on the left-hand side of the organizer, begin attaching the bias binding. As you bind the top of the organizer, stitch in all four pieces of elastic. Before you reach the right-hand bottom corner, stretch the pieces of elastic across the organizer and pin to the appropriate marks along the bottom edge; this will cause the organizer to curl. Finish binding the organizer, catching the elastic as you bind the bottom edge.

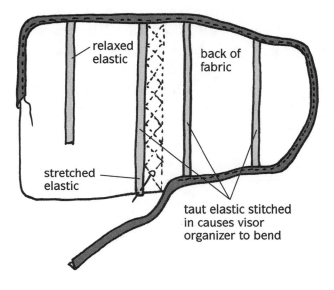

relaxed elastic

back of fabric

stretched elastic

taut elastic stitched in causes visor organizer to bend

12 *To use* with the visor in the down position, unclip your car's sun visor, slide organizer over visor with the elastic facing the windshield, and reclip. Flip visor down to insert items or up to conceal. The organizer will lay flat against the sun visor.

Passport Pouch

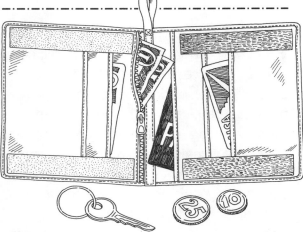

This slim bifold wallet is designed to hold your passport, money, and credit cards. It has a hanging loop made of twill tape or grosgrain ribbon, so that you can conceal it beneath your clothes while traveling. If you want to hang the passport pouch around your neck, you can use a longer piece of twill tape or ribbon to make a much larger loop. I recommend using a soft fabric, if it will be next to your skin, or a light-weight nylon so it doesn't add weight to your baggage. Think about using a more decorative fabric for the cover, and a durable fabric for the inner lining and pockets.

Materials

¼ yard sturdy light-weight fabric, 36" wide
1–2 yards double-fold bias tape, ¼" wide
6" hook and loop fastener, ½" wide
One 5" or 6" zipper (nylon coil recommended)
10" (or more) light-weight twill tape or grosgrain
    ribbon, ½" wide (for looping onto a belt); or
    30" or more, ½" wide (to hang around neck)
Sewing thread

CUTTING LAYOUT

Fold the fabric in half, selvage to selvage, right sides together. If you use a different fabric for the outer cover (piece **A2**), cut only the pouch liner (piece **A1**) out of the folded fabric.

    Following the measurements and layout shown, draw the pieces on the fabric and cut out.

The pieces in this project are:

A1 and **A2.** Pouch liner and outer cover, 8½" wide x 5½" long

B. Passport pocket, 4" wide x 5½" long

C. Zipper pocket, 4" wide x 5½" long (note that pieces **B** and **C** are the same size)

D. Credit card pocket with hem, 4¾" wide x 3" long

E. Credit card pocket without hem, 4¾" wide x 3" long

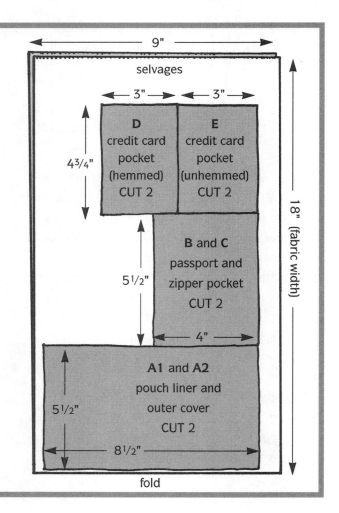

Making the Pockets

1 Bind one long edge (top) on the passport pocket (**B**), credit card pocket with hem (**D**), and credit card pocket without hem (**E**) (five pieces total).

2 On both of the hemmed credit card pocket pieces (**D**), clip the lower corners and turn under and press 1/2" along the bottom edge. On all four credit card pocket pieces (**D** and **E**), turn under and press 1/2" along both *side* edges.

3 Turn under and press 1/2" along one long edge of the zipper pocket (**C**).

4 Pin one hemmed credit card pocket (**D**) to the passport pocket (**B**), 1/2" from the bound edge, centered. Topstitch, 1/8" in from the edge, along the bottom of the hemmed credit card pocket (**D**). Pin one unhemmed credit card pocket (**E**) to the passport pocket (**B**) 1/2" below the hemmed credit card pocket. Stitch 1/8" in from the edges, along the sides of the two credit card pockets (**D** and **E**).

5 Pin the other hemmed credit card pocket (**D**) to the zipper pocket (**C**), 1/2" from the turned edge, centered. Topstitch, 1/8" in from the edge, along the bottom of the hemmed credit card pocket (**D**). Pin one unhemmed credit card pocket (**E**) to the zipper pocket (**C**) 1/2" below the hemmed credit card pocket (**D**). Stitch 1/8" in from the edges, along the sides of the two credit card pockets.

Attaching the Zipper and Hook and Loop

6 Stitch the turned edge of the zipper pocket (**C**) to one side of the zipper (see page 35), close to the zipper teeth.

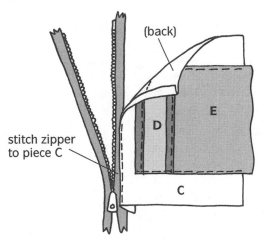

7 Cut the 6" piece of hook and loop in half. Pin both 3" pieces of the hook side of the fastener to the zipper pocket (**C**), along the sides of the credit card pockets, starting just below the zipper stitching. Pin both pieces of the loop side of the fastener to the passport pocket (**B**), along the sides of the credit card pockets, starting just below the binding edge. Make sure there is 1/4" border all the way

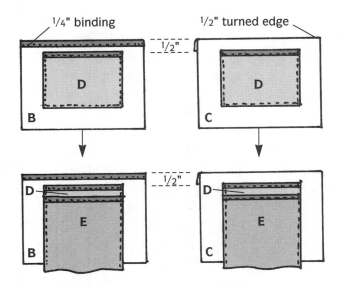

around the pouch. If not, trim the ¹/₂" wide hook and loop to ³/₈" to allow for a ¹/₄" fabric border.

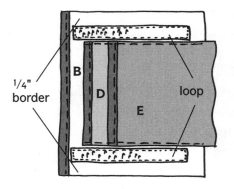

Putting It All Together

8 Draw a line on the face side of the pouch liner (**A1**), 3¹/₂" in from one end of the 8¹/₂" edges. Line up the zipper teeth of the zpper pocket (**C**) along this line. Stitching close to the zipper teeth, attach the other side of the zipper to the pouch liner (**A1**).

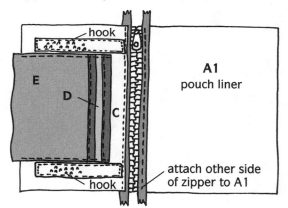

9 Place the passport pocket (**B**) on the other side of the pouch liner (**A1**), lining up the raw edges. Using ¹/₈" seam allowance, stitch all around the pouch liner, catching the edges of the zipper tape and passport pockets.

Adding the Outer Cover

10 Lay the inner pouch assembly on top of the wrong side of the outer cover (**A2**) and, using ¹/₈" seam allowance, stitch

together carefully, rounding the corners of the pouch as you stitch. Trim the outer edges of the pouch so that all of the layers are flush.

11 Starting at the center of the long end of the pouch, on the side where the zipper pull is located when the zipper is shut, bind the outer edges of the pouch (see page 29). The unfinished edges of the binding will be covered by the twill tape or ribbon loop.

Attaching the Hanging Loop

12 Press under ¹/₂" on both ends of the piece of tape or ribbon (this length will vary if you plan to hang the pouch around your neck). Pin one end to the inside of the pouch, centered, just above the binding on the edge opposite the zipper pull. Continue pinning the tape so that it covers the zipper tape and makes a nice finish along the center of the pouch. Using a very tiny seam allowance, stitch all the way around the tape. Now flip the remaining tape back under itself, leaving a 2" long loop (or longer for neck strap).

13 Make a box stitch on the loop side of the tape, starting just under the binding, and stitching through all layers. This tape treatment serves many purposes — it covers the zipper tape, causes the pouch to hinge nicely at the center, and forms the hanging loop.

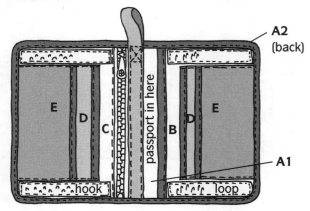

five

Basic Bags: Shapes that Hold Things

- *Vegetable Keeper*
- *Jelly Bag*
- *Laundry Bag*
- *Stuff Sack*
- *Grocery Bag*
- *Water Bottle Shoulder Bag*
- *Garment Bag*

I've been playing with bag designs for years, and I've had both successes and failures! A brief tour through local stores (or your own closet) will give you an idea of just how much variation there can be in bag construction. This chapter offers several techniques for making different types of bags. It begins by describing how to make the most basic flat bag, and then, by adding casings of different types and sizes, gives you the skills to modify the bag concept for an infinite variety of uses.

I have deliberately tried to keep these projects simple, emphasizing only the bag, handle, and closure features, so that you can embellish them in your own way. Once you know the basics — how to make drawstring, tote, and zippered bags — you can customize and create bags for any use.

Vegetable Keeper

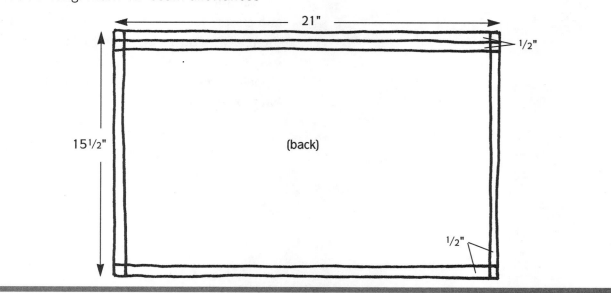

A vegetable keeper is an example of a hemmed flat bag. It is made of cloth, which helps fresh vegetables stay fresh longer, because they can breathe, and the fabric absorbs excess moisture. The instructions here are for a vegetable keeper bag with a finished measurement of 10" wide x 14" long.

Flat-hemmed bags can be used in countless ways. Make them from velvet for gift bags; use country calico to make bags for storing matching calico napkins and tablecloths. This is a great project to teach kids how to sew something useful.

Materials

½ yard 100 percent cotton cheesecloth, gauze, or coarse muslin, at least 21" wide
Sewing thread

Cutting Layout

Following the measurements and layout shown, draw a rectangle 21" wide x 15½" long. Mark ½" seam allowances along the sides and bottom. Mark two ½" hem lines along the top. Cut out the rectangle.

21"

½"

15½"

(back)

½"

Constructing the Bag

1 Press under ¹/₂" twice along the top edge, for the hem. Using a ¹/₈" seam allowance, stitch the turned inner edge.

2 Fold the bag in half, right sides together, with the side edges lined up. Using a ¹/₂" seam allowance, stitch down the side seam, pivot around the bottom corner, and stitch the bottom closed. Press the seams open and turn right-side out. The vegetable keeper can be folded or twisted shut, or tied closed with a string or twist-tie.

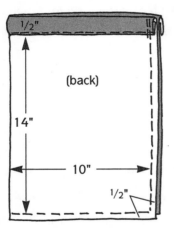

VARIATION: SACHET BAG

Sachet bags are tied closed below the top edge, leaving a gathered top. To ensure that the back of the fabric will not show along the inside top edge, you need to make the top hem wider. For a sachet bag with a finished size of 3 x 6", add two 1" turns to make the top hem. This will require a 7" wide x 8½" long piece of fabric.

To construct a Sachet Bag, follow steps 1 and 2 in the main project instructions. Using a 7 to 9" length of ribbon, gather the top of the bag together, and tie a bow. If you are concerned that the contents might escape, close the bag with a rubber band, then conceal it under the ribbon tie.

CUSTOMIZING BAG SIZES

To decide on the size of the piece of fabric needed to make a specific bag, first determine the finished size of the bag you wish to make: width (**a**) and length (**b**). To determine the width of the fabric piece, double measurement (**a**) and add 1" (for ¹/₂" side seam allowances). To determine the length of the fabric, add ¹/₂" to measurement (**b**) for the bottom seam allowance, and, as well, add enough material to make a doubled hem of whatever width you choose along the top.

Jelly Bag

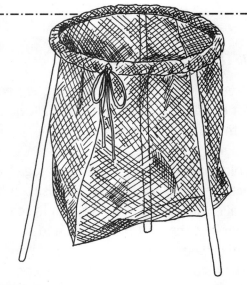

This is an example of a basic drawstring bag with a flap casing. In a flap-casing construction, the side seam ends below the casing, leaving the casing ends open for the drawstring to exit. A jelly bag is constructed of loosely woven fabric. It allows fruit juice to filter through its threads but is strong enough to be hung from a metal ring or a hook. Companies that make canning jars generally sell the metal ring stands with bags, but the bags wear out. Being able to make your own is one benefit of practical sewing.

The instructions here are for a 9" jelly bag with rounded bottom corners, that hangs from a 6¼" diameter metal ring.

Materials

19 x 11" (or larger) piece loosely woven plain-weave fabric (cheesecloth, gauze, coarse muslin, or other)
Household string
Small safety pin
Sewing thread

Cutting Layout

Following the measurements and layout shown, draw a rectangle 19" wide x 11" long. Mark ½" seam allowance along the bottom and sides. (If you want a rounded bag, sketch a rounded line along the bottom corners, with ½" seam allowance all around). Mark ½" line, then two 1" lines below that along the top edge.

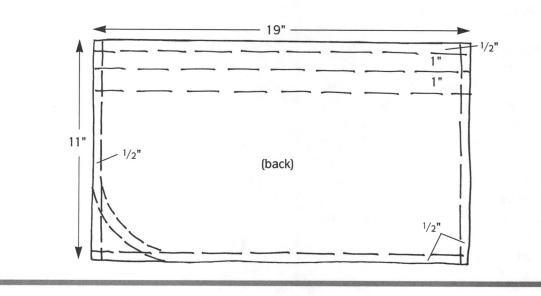

Constructing the Bag

1 Fold the bag in half, right sides together, with the side edges lined up. Using ½" seam allowance, stitch the side and bottom seams, starting at the line that is 2½" down from the top edge, and pivoting around corners.

2 Press open the bottom and side seam allowances, making sure to press open the ½" at the top, where there is no seam. Stitch ¼" in from the fold, around this open seam allowance, from the top edge to ¼" below the start of the seam. Stitch across the bottom of the opening and then back up the other side to the top edge, pivoting at the corners.

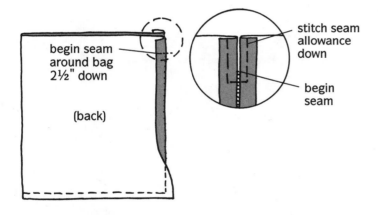

begin seam around bag 2½" down

(back)

stitch seam allowance down

begin seam

3 Press under ½" and then 1" along the top edge to make the hem. The folded edge will lie along the third (last) 1" marked line. Topstitch close to the folded edge, backstitching at both ends of the casing.

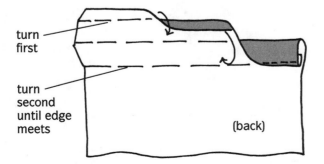

turn first

turn second until edge meets

(back)

4 Tie the string to the safety pin, and thread it through the casing and all the way around. Tie the ends of the string together.

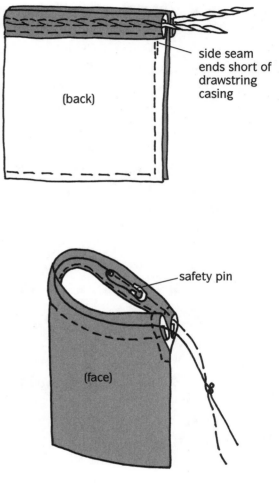

(back)

side seam ends short of drawstring casing

safety pin

(face)

Laundry Bag

This is an example of a slot-casing drawstring bag — the most clean-finished of the casing constructions. The casing is a fully enclosed hem, with a slot sewn in it for the drawstring to exit. You can use this construction for any fabrication, although it is difficult to do with particularly narrow casings and small bags. You can make a slot-casing drawstring bag out of nylon mesh to use for camping gear — fill it with dirty dishes and put it in the river to rinse them! To create a laundry hamper, hang the bag over a box or frame, pulling the drawstring taut around the top opening. This project uses a 1" casing with the drawstring exiting on the outside (see Slot Casings box, page 81).

Materials

1¼ yards sturdy fabric, 45" wide (poplin, gabardine, ripstop nylon, or a nylon mesh — which will prevent damp clothes from mildewing)
Large grommet (optional)
2 yards heavy drawstring
Safety pin
Sewing thread

Cutting Layout

Fold the fabric in half, selvage to selvage, right sides together. Following the measurements and layout shown, draw one 21" wide x 38" long rectangles and cut out. On the back of the fabric, mark two ½" seam allowances along the left side of one rectangle and the right side of the other rectangle. Mark one ½" seam allowance along the other side and bottom of each rectangle. Mark ½", then two 1" casing fold lines along the top edges of both rectangles. On the sides with the two ½" seam allowances, within the lower 1" casing border, draw two points, one ⅛" from the top, the other ⅛" from the bottom. Draw a ¾" line (slot) connecting the two points along the seam allowance, centered within the 1" border. (If you want to make slots for a double drawstring,

similar to the Bandana Bundle, page 48, mark slots and a double seam allowance on both side edges of both rectangles.)

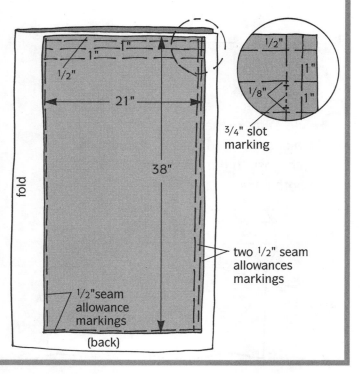

two ½" seam allowances markings

¾" slot marking

½"seam allowance markings

(back)

fold

Constructing the Bag

1 With right sides together, line up the two sides with the slot markings. Stitch along the second side seam from the top edge down to the top of the ³/₄" centered slot, and backstitch. Start stitching again, beginning at the lower mark of the ³/₄" slot (backstitching at the beginning of the seam), and sew the rest of the side.

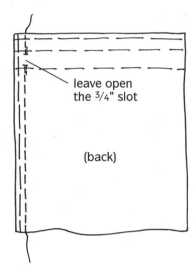

leave open the ³/₄" slot

(back)

2 Turn under and press ¹/₂" along the first seam allowance on both sides of the slotted side seam. Then, choose one of the the following options:

a. Stitch these seam allowances down to the main body of the bag, close to their folded edges, along the entire length of the bag.

b. Stitch the seam allowances down along the casing only.

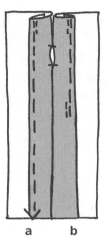

a   b

3 To finish the slot, you also have two options:

a. Stitch a rectangle around the entire slot.

b. Attach a grommet directly over the slot, centered on the seam line.

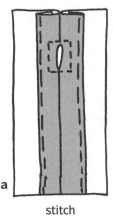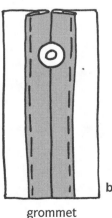

a   b

stitch   grommet

SLOT CASINGS

In general, when you design a slot casing, you need to mark ¹/₂" hem at the top to be turned under, and then mark two strips the desired width of the casing below the ¹/₂" hem. The upper strip will become the inside of the casing; the lower strip will become the outside of the casing. Decide which side of the casing you want the drawstring to exit from, and center the marks for the slot opening in the appropriate strip (upper or lower), making sure it is wide enough to hold your chosen drawstring material.

4 Using ¹/₂" seam allowance, stitch the opposite side seam, pivot around the bottom corner, and continue stitching the bottom closed. To ensure a secure corner on the other side, pivot and stitch part way up the other (already sewn) side.

5 On the top edge, press under ¹/₂", then 1" twice to form the casing. Lay the bag on the sewing machine so that the inner casing edge is facing up, and sew along the circular casing, stitching close to the inner casing edge.

6 Fasten the cord to the safety pin, and thread it through and all the way around the casing. Leave the drawstring ends as long as you desire and finish in one of the following ways:

a. Tie the ends together.

b. Thread the ends through a toggle clamp or cord lock.

c. For more decorative applications, thread one or more beads onto the strings before knotting them (separately or together).

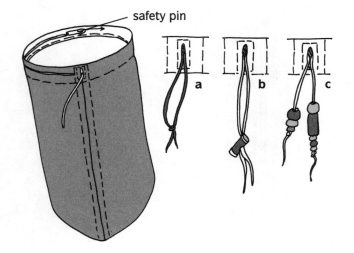

safety pin

Stuff Sack

A stuff sack is a tubular bag with a draw-string casing and a round inner flap that covers the contents before the drawstring casing is cinched. They are commonly used for storing sleeping bags, although you can make them for any round or rollable item, such as a blanket you store in the car, or a patio umbrella and poles. The instructions here are for a stuff sack 18" tall with an 8" diameter base.

Materials

⅔ yard fabric, 54" wide (nylon taffeta, ripstop nylon, or other)
1 yard durable drawstring (round nylon, ¼" diameter)
Toggle clamp or cord lock (optional))
Sewing thread

Cutting Layout

Starting with a single layer of fabric, fold in one selvage 11" in order to cut two of pattern pieces **A** and **C** from the folded goods. Following the measurements and layout shown, draw the pieces on the fabric, using a compass to draw the circular pieces, and cut out (also see box, "How to Make Large Circles,"

page 47 for another method to draw the sack bottom and inner-lid pieces).

The pieces in this project are:

A. Sack bottom, 9" diameter circle
B. Sack wall, 26⅛" wide x 20" long
C. Inner lid, 10" diameter circle

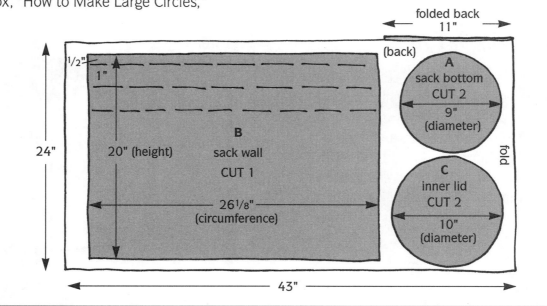

Making the Casing

1 Mark a line ¹/₂" from the top edge of the sack wall; then mark a line 1" below the previous, and mark another 1" below that.

2 Fold the sack wall in half, right sides together, lining up the edges. Using ¹/₂" seam allowance, stitch the side seam of the sack wall, starting right below the last casing fold line. Press open the seam. Topstitch the seam allowances down from the top edge to the last casing fold line.

3 Press under ¹/₂", then 1" on the casing. Stitch the casing ¹/₈" from the inner turned edge. Restitch close to the outer folded edge, using a ¹/₈" seam allowance.

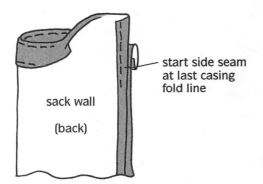

start side seam at last casing fold line

sack wall

(back)

Adding the Inner Lid

4 Using ¹/₂" seam allowance, stitch the two inner lid pieces together, right sides facing, leaving a small opening for turning. Turn right side out and press. Slipstitch the opening closed. Topstitch close to the edge, around the entire inner lid. Turn the sack wall to be inside out.

5 Fold the sack wall tube in half and mark the point directly opposite the casing opening. Catch a 1" section of the lid in a seam of the same length; this seam will connect the lid to the bag along the lower seam of the casing. Stitch several times.

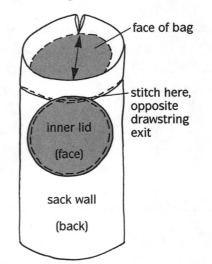

face of bag

stitch here, opposite drawstring exit

inner lid

(face)

sack wall

(back)

Attaching the Bottom

6 Pin the two sack bottom pieces together, wrong sides facing, and treat as one piece. Pin the sack bottom to the right side of the sack wall tube as illustrated. With the sack wall tube facing you, use ¹/₂" seam allowance to sew the sack bottom to the sack wall tube, being careful not to catch large tucks of fabric in the seam. You may, however, need to make small tucks as you stitch around the circle in order to fit the two pieces together.

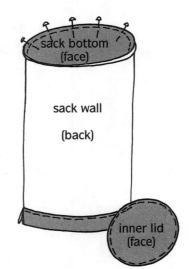

sack bottom
(face)

sack wall

(back)

inner lid
(face)

7 Tie the cord to the safety pin, and thread it through and around the casing. Thread both ends of the drawstring into a cord lock, if desired (this will enable you to tightly cinch the stuff sack closed).

VARIATION: USING GROMMETS INSTEAD OF A DRAWSTRING

Instead of making a drawstring casing, make a full hem around the top, by turning the fabric down ¾" and then another ¾", and stitching close to the inside folded edge (so that there will be three complete layers of fabric throughout the hem). Attach an odd number of grommets at logical intervals around the hem, and thread the drawstring in and out of the grommet holes, so that both ends exit toward either the inside or the outside of the bag. You can then thread the ends of the drawstring into a cord lock.

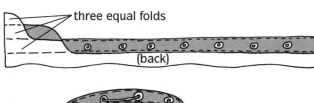
three equal folds
(back)

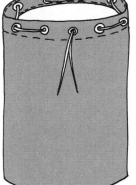

CUSTOMIZING THE STUFF SACK

You can make the Stuff Sack as indicated in these instructions, or you can customize it to fit a specific item.

- **To determine the diameter** of the sack bottom, measure the diameter of the item for which you are making the sack, and add at least ¹/₂", so that the sack is not too snug, and another 1", for the ¹/₂" seam allowance on both sides.

- **To determine the height** of the sack wall, measure the height of the item, add ¹/₂" seam allowance to the top and bottom, plus 1" for the flap casing (see Jelly Bag, page 78, for details).

- **To determine the circumference** of the sack (which is also the width of the sack wall), use the following formula:

  $C = \pi \times d$ (circumference equals π times the diameter; π = 3.14)

  Translated, this means that the circumference equals 3.14 x the diameter of the circle you started with (before adding seam allowances, but after adding the extra ¹/₂" for ease). Therefore, first compute the circumference, then add 1" for the side seam allowances, to get the width of the sack wall.

  To determine the inner lid measurement, add 2" to the finished diameter measurement.

Grocery Bag

This basic rectangular tote bag features a double-reinforced bottom. The reinforcement piece fits the bottom and has triangular extensions that mimic the triangular folds of a real paper grocery sack. The bag also has a strap webbing handle that extends all the way around the bottom of the bag, allowing you to carry extra-heavy groceries without tearing the seams. I recommend making this tote out of a heavier fabric such as canvas, heavy twill, or pack cloth. A vinyl laminate is also a good choice for the bottom reinforcement, since it is water repellent.

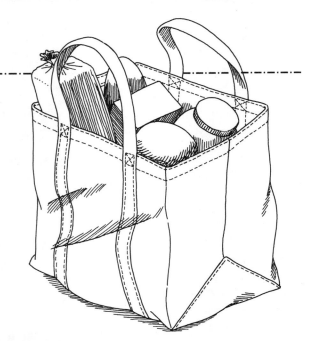

Materials

1½ yards fabric, 60" wide (2 yards, if narrower)
2½ yards cotton or nylon strap webbing, 1" wide
2 yards double-fold bias binding, ½" wide
Sewing thread

Cutting Layout

Following the measurements and layout shown, draw the pieces on the fabric and cut out.

The pattern pieces in this project are:

A. Bag body, 51" wide x 46" long

B. Bottom reinforcement, 21" wide x 8" long

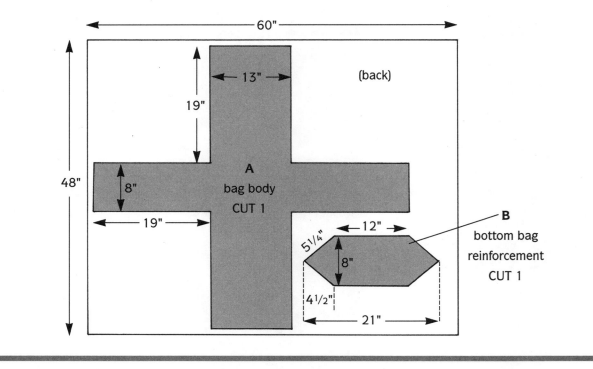

Reinforcing the Bottom

1 Turn under and press ½" on all sides of the bottom reinforcement piece. Pin the wrong side of the bottom reinforcement to the right side of the bag body, so that it fits just inside the seam allowances of the bag body. Stitch ⅛" from the edge all the way around the reinforcement piece.

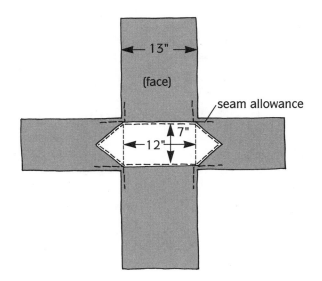

Hemming the Top Edges

2 Turn under 1" twice on all of the hemlines of the bag body (the four cross ends). Measure each side of the cross shape to be sure they are all 17". Stitch all four hems

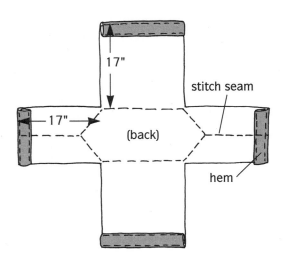

⅛" in from the inner turned edge, and again at ⅛" in from the outer edge. With chalk, mark a straight line from both triangle points of the bottom reinforcement piece out to the center of the narrower bag sides. Stitch along these lines through the hems. This stitch line will help the bag to fold just like a grocery bag.

Attaching the Strap Webbing

3 With chalk, mark lines 2" in from the edges of the wider bag sides, running the full length (across the bottom reinforcement). Starting at the center of the cross (the bottom of the bag), pin the strap webbing to these lines, so that it's outer edge runs along the chalk lines. When you reach the hems, make 12" loops for the handles, being sure not to twist the webbing. Once you return to the starting point, turn under 1 inch of webbing and pin it over the raw edge.

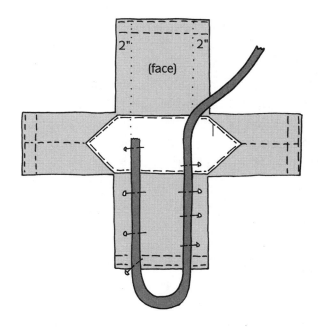

4 Stitch ⅛" in from both edges of the webbing. Make box stitches at the webbing join seam and at the four points where the straps meet the hems.

Before reaching the bottom corner, turn under the binding edge and backstitch it in place. Repeat for the other three side seams.

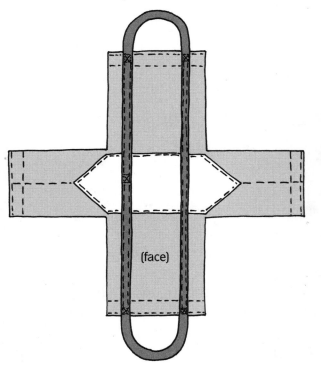

(face)

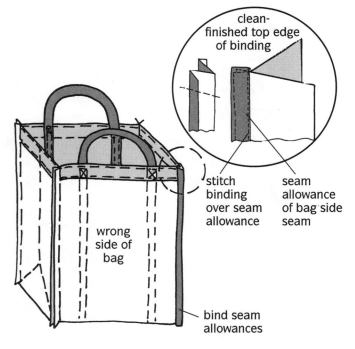

clean-finished top edge of binding

stitch binding over seam allowance

seam allowance of bag side seam

wrong side of bag

bind seam allowances

Stitching and Binding the Side Seams

5 Pin together adjacent sides of the cross, right sides together, to form four side seams. Using a ½" seam allowance, sew all four seams so that the top hems meet flush at the top of the bag, and the bottom corners meet at the finished edges of the bottom reinforcement. Trim the seam allowances to ¼".

6 Cut four 18" pieces of bias binding. On one end of each piece, with right sides together, stitch across the binding ¼" in from the end. Turn and press right-side out. Place one of these finished binding ends around the top edge of one of the four side seam allowances, and stitch the rest of the binding close to the edge, over the seam allowance.

DESIGN AND DECORATING OPTIONS

This project is a good one for testing your new pattern-making knowledge and embellishment skills.

✂ There are many ways to construct tote bags, and even more variations in design. Look at bags in stores to analyze their construction and get new ideas; and experiment with sizes and shapes. One variation is to line the bag by cutting two of piece A and stitching the top edges of each together (using 2" seam allowances) instead of hemming them.

✂ Add pockets, for your coupon holder and grocery list.

✂ Decorate the bag with painted motifs, embroidery, or different trims and bric-a-brac.

Water Bottle Shoulder Bag

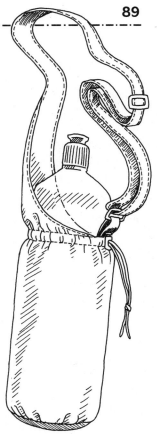

This round bag is made to fit perfectly around your favorite water bottle. The instructions given are for a bag with a shoulder strap cut as part of the body fabric. If you want to make an insulated bag, cut the outer shell larger than the lining to allow room for the padding. A nylon pack cloth fabric for the outer shell with a thin waterproof lining is a good combination. You might also choose a more decorative outer fabric, with a lining that resists water absorption, such as nylon taffeta. If you are using a fabric with a sticky finish, sew with tissue paper under the fabric to prevent it from sticking to the stitch plate, and tear off the tissue after you sew. If you choose heavy or thick fabrics, you will need to modify the strap width to 3" instead of 2" so that you are able to turn the narrow strap right-side out. The instructions here are for a Water Bottle Shoulder Bag that will hold a water bottle 8" high, with a diameter of 3¼", and a circumference of 10¼".

Materials

Water bottle

Outer cover and lining fabrics: ⅓ to ½ yard fabric 60" wide; or 60" each fabric, 12–18" wide (if using different fabrics for outer cover and lining). Lay outer cover and lining fabrics on top of one another and pin to prevent slipping. Cut pattern pieces out as if one piece.

One 1" D ring

One slider buckle, 1" wide

3" piece strap webbing or heavy twill tape, 1" wide

Cord (length should be at least 12" longer than the circumference of bottle), ⅛ – ³⁄₁₆" thick

Small safety pin

Cord lock (optional)

½" double-fold bias binding, ½" wide (length equal to the circumference of bottle plus 2"

Sewing thread

Cutting Layout

Following the measurements and layout shown, draw the pieces on the fabric, mark, and cut out (use a compass or see box, "How to Mark Large Circles," page 47 to draw the bag bottom).

The pieces in this project are:

A. Water bottle, 11 3/4" wide (circumference) x 7 3/4" long (height) with strap (see below)

B. Bag bottom, 4 1/4" diameter circle

To draw the strap: Find the center along one long edge of the rectangle, and mark. Measure out 2" from each side of this point, and draw two lines extending up for 10", 4" apart. Then, find the center of this 4" wide length of the strap, measure out 1 1/2" from either side of this center point, and draw two lines extending up for 10", 3" apart (you are tapering the strap from 4" to 3" wide). Find the center of this 3" wide length of the strap, measure out 1" from either side of this center point, and draw two lines extending up for the remaining 25" of the strap (you are tapering the strap from 3" to 2" wide). Draw a line across to connect these two lines. Round the inside corners where the strap meets the rectangle.

Once you have drawn your fabric patterns, cut one of each from the lining fabric, and one of each from the outer shell fabric. Mark the 1/2" seam allowances on the wrong side of the fabric. On the water bottle piece, mark the drawstring casing lines in chalk on the right side of the outer cover fabric, along the top edge of the rectangle, 1/8" and 3/4" in from the 1/2" seam allowance.

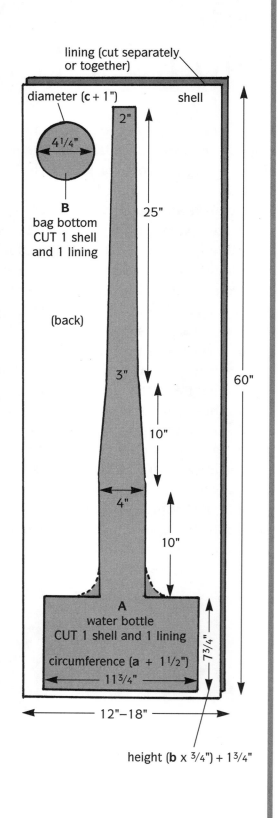

lining (cut separately or together)

diameter (c + 1")

shell

4 1/4"

B
bag bottom
CUT 1 shell
and 1 lining

2"

25"

(back)

3"

10"

4"

10"

60"

A
water bottle
CUT 1 shell and 1 lining

circumference (a + 1 1/2")

11 3/4"

7 3/4"

12"–18"

height (b x 3/4") + 1 3/4"

CUSTOMIZING THE WATER BOTTLE SHOULDER BAG

You can make the Water Bottle Shoulder Bag as indicated in these instructions, or you can customize it to fit a specific water bottle.

In order to determine the pattern dimensions, you must first take the measurements of the water bottle you are making the cover for. Measure the circumference of the bottle at its widest point (**a**); measure the height of the bottle, from the base to the neck (**b**); and measure the diameter of the base of the bottle (**c**).

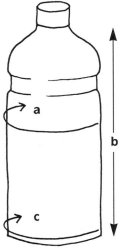

The main pattern piece is a rectangle. To determine the length of the rectangle, take the circumference of the bottle (**a**) and add 1/2" ease to fit the bottle, and 1/2" seam allowances on each end (1 1/2" total). To determine the width of this piece, take 3/4 the height of the bottle (**b**), and add 3/4" for the drawstring casing, plus 1/2" seam allowances on each end (1 3/4" total). (The strap of this main pattern piece will be drawn as described in the cutting layout, page 90).

The other pattern piece is the bag bottom. To determine the diameter of the circle, take the diameter of the base of the bottle (**c**), and add 1/2" seam allowance all around (1" total to diameter).

Lining the Bag

1 Fold the lining in half, right sides together, with the side edges lined up. Using 1/2" seam allowance, stitch the side seam of the lining, to make a circle.

2 Fold the outer shell fabric in half, right sides together, with the side edges lined up. Using 1/2" seam allowance, stitch the side seam of the outer fabric, leaving a slot opening between the drawstring casing lines. Backstitch at both ends of the slot opening. Press open the seam allowance, and stitch a rectangle around the slot twice, backstitching to secure the seam. This will reinforce the drawstring slot.

3 With right sides facing, place the outer sleeve inside the lining. Thread the D ring onto the 3" length of webbing, and fold it in half. Pin the strap loop at the side seam, between the two layers of fabric, with all raw edges lined up. Using 1/2" seam allowance, stitch around the upper edge of the rectangles and all around the entire length of the shoulder strap, pivoting at the corners.

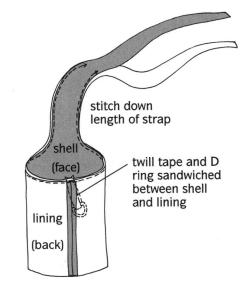

Clip the corners, curves, and seam allowances. Turn the entire bag inside out, by pulling the strap through itself until it is right-side out. A chopstick or thin dowel can be used to push in and pull the inner fabric to the outside.

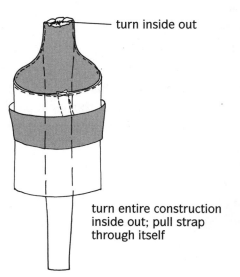

turn inside out

turn entire construction inside out; pull strap through itself

4 Press the sewn seams so that the fabrics lay flat. Topstitch close to the edge, around the top of the rectangle and all the way around the strap.

Threading the Drawstring and Strap

5 The topstitching operation in step 4 will become the top edge of the drawstring casing. Complete the casing top edge by sewing a line of stitching below the strap that connects the topstitching around the rectangle. Stitch the lower drawstring casing line, sewing along the previously marked chalk line. It is easiest to stitch along the inside of the bag.

6 Tie the cord to the safety pin, and thread it through and all the way around the inside of the casing. Thread both ends of the drawstring into a cord lock, if desired.

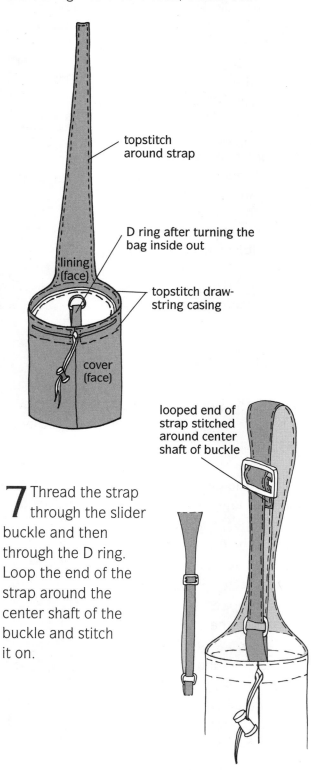

topstitch around strap

D ring after turning the bag inside out

lining (face)

topstitch draw-string casing

cover (face)

looped end of strap stitched around center shaft of buckle

7 Thread the strap through the slider buckle and then through the D ring. Loop the end of the strap around the center shaft of the buckle and stitch it on.

Attaching the Bottom

8 Turn the bag inside out. Pin the two bag bottoms together, wrong sides facing, and treat them as one piece. Pin the bag bottom to the bag, matching the lining fabric and the outer shell fabric, with the seam allowance on the inside of the bag. Using 1/2" seam allowance, stitch the bottom onto the bag.

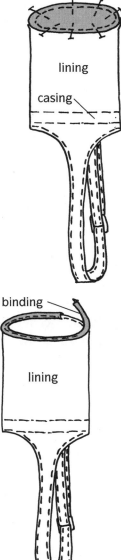

9 Trim the seam allowances to 1/4". Bind around the entire bottom seam allowance (see page 29).

10 *To use,* turn the bag right-side out, pop the bottle into the bag, adjust the strap length, and you're ready for an outing!

DESIGN OPTIONS

✂ If you don't want to make the strap an integral part of the pattern, make a Stuff Sack (see page 83) to fit the dimensions of your bottle, and attach strap webbing to make the shoulder strap.

✂ The drawstring is an optional feature, and can be omitted. However, if your bottle tapers significantly toward the top, the drawstring is important — it cinches and locks at a narrower part of the bottle, and ensures a tight fit. Without a drawstring, the bag would be loose ¾ of the way up.

✂ Don't limit yourself to covering water bottles; the basic concept can be expanded to make a cover for any vessel you want to carry over your shoulder. For example, following the same basic instructions outlined in this project, you can make a cover with a built-in strap for a plastic bucket. Instead of a drawstring, insert a piece of stiff wire or a steel ring into the casing to shape the bucket cover and hold open the top. Or, make a heavy canvas bucket with a strap.

Garment Bag

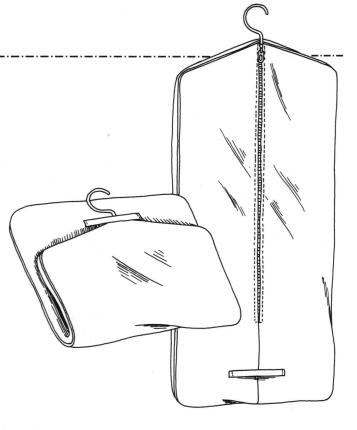

This hanging garment bag is designed to hold one or two garments. It measures 22" wide x 36" long and is hung by the garment hanger. This garment bag has a zippered-front, and a piped outer seam that helps to keep its shape as it hangs in a closet or in a car. Once completed, you can hang the garment bag up fully open, or fold it in half, thread the hanger through the hanger loop (to hold the bottom of the bag), and hang it up in the folded position.

Many different fabrics can be used in the construction of this bag. Select something sufficiently smooth so the clothing slides easily into the bag, rather than bunching up. For outdoor use, choose a water-repellent fabric. I used a tightly woven polyester/cotton gabardine, about 6 ounces per square yard.

Materials

2½ yards fabric, at least 48" wide
    (2 yards, if 54" or wider)
4 yards welting cord, ⅛–⅜" thick
30" zipper
Hanger
Sewing thread

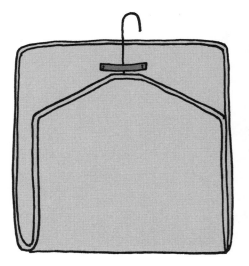

Cutting Layout

I based this pattern on a standard-sized coat hanger I found in my closet. If your hanger differs significantly, you may need to modify the angle at the top of the bag to better fit your hanger.

Fold the fabric in half, selvage to selvage, right sides together. Following the measurements and layout shown, draw the pieces on the fabric, mark, and cut out.

The pieces in this project are:

A. Bag front, 12" wide x 38" long

B. Bag back, 11 1/2" wide x 38" long

C. Continuous strip bias binding, 1 1/2" wide x 4 yards long (see page 28)

D. Hanger loop (optional), 3" wide x 4" long

On the bag front, mark a point 8" down on the nonselvage edge, and connect it to a point 1/2" over from the selvage along the 12" edge. Measure down 1" from this point, and draw a line from the edge of the fabric to the diagonal line. Cut along these lines to form the top of the bag.

On the bag back, mark a point on the nonfolded long edge, 8" down. Connect this point to the corner on the fold of the 11 1/2" top. Measure down 1" from this point, and draw a line from the edge of the fabric to the diagonal line. Cut along these lines.

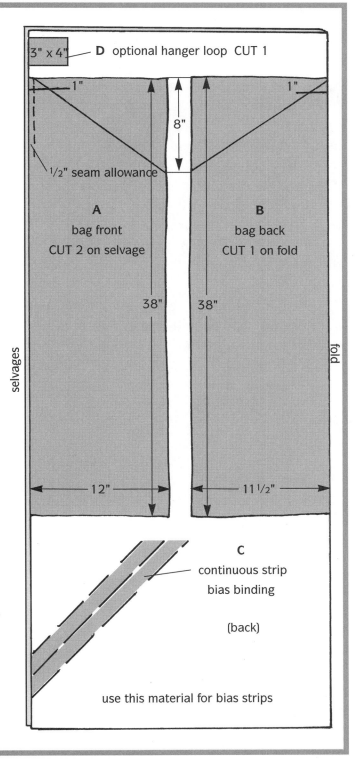

Attaching the Zipper

1 Using ¹/2" seam allowance, baste the selvage edges of the two bag fronts together, right sides facing. Measure 6¹/2" from the bottom of the bag, mark, and restitch this last 6¹/2" along the seam line using a normal stitch count.

2 Press the seam allowances open. Lay the zipper down with the tab facing the pressed out seam allowances, and the zipper top located 1¹/2" down from the raw edge of the top of the bag triangle.

3 Using a zipper foot, sew on the zipper (see page 34), and open the basted seam to expose the zipper teeth.

the bottom edge, centered, and stitch ¹/8" and again ¹/4" from the edge, along the two turned edges.

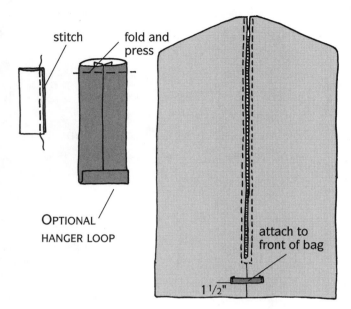

stitch   fold and press

OPTIONAL HANGER LOOP

attach to front of bag

1¹/2"

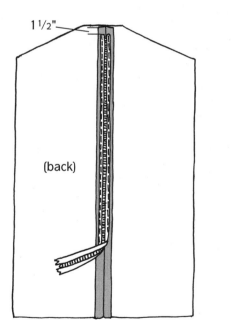

1¹/2"

(back)

4 Fold the hanger loop (optional) in half, right sides together, and, using ¹/2" seam allowance, stitch along the 4" edges. Turn right-side out and press, with the seam centered. Press under ¹/2" at each end. Place the loop on the bag front, 1¹/2" up from

Making and Attaching the Welting

5 After making the continuous strip bias binding, use the zipper foot to enclose the welting cord inside the strip (see page 32). Trim the raw edges of the welting cord to ¹/2" width. Leave 6" of cord and fabric strip unsewn at one end.

6 Starting at the bottom, pin the welting to the bag back, lining the raw edges, and leaving the unsewn section of the welting hanging loose. Begin stitching the sewn section of the welting to the bag, stitching just inside the welting seam line. At each corner, stitch until you reach ¹/2" from the edge with the needle in the down position, raise the presser foot, and clip the seam allowance of the welting to allow it to open and curve easier. Pivot around the corners, and continue sewing. When you reach 6" from the starting point, backstitch a few stitches and end the seam.

7 To join the welting ends, leave enough welting to overlap the starting (unsewn) strip by at least 6". Mark, in chalk, on both pieces of welting, the point where the two ends would comfortably intersect. Open the bias fabric seam on both pieces several inches inside these points. Lay the two pieces of strip bias binding at right angles, right sides together, so that the chalk points match exactly. Pin in place and pull the strips open to be sure that they are pinned properly. Stitch the diagonal (mitered) seam across the right angle. Clip the welting cord so that the two ends meet at a different point than the seam you just sewed. Start sewing at the backstitching point from step 6, and continue until you reach the starting point. The entire bag back will now be surrounded in welting (see page 31).

Finishing the Bag

8 Pin the bag front to the bag back, right sides together, carefully pinning the center seam edges above the zipper so they meet and will not gap open when stitched to the backing. Match all angled corners. Position the bag so that the bag back is facing up and you can see the seam that joined the welting. Using a zipper foot, start at the bottom of the bag, and stitch the bag front to the bag back just inside the welt join seam. The zipper foot should hug the welting tightly. As you sew, make sure that the raw edges of the bag front stay flush with the edges of the bag back. As you pivot the corners, make sure that the welting is pushed to the inside of the seam.

9 Unzip the zipper, and turn the bag right-side out. Press carefully along the welting to set the seam to the inside and the welt to the outside.

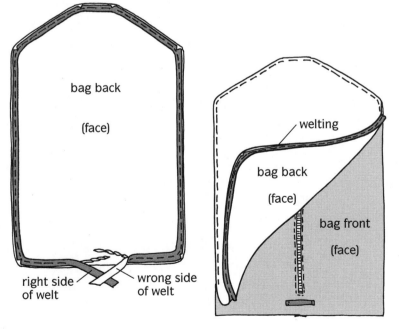

six

Sew Storage: Three-Dimensional Pockets

- *Hanging Shoe Rack*
- *Bucket Caddy*
- *Carpenter's Half-Apron*
- *Traveling Jewelry Bag*

By **combining the different** bag and pocket techniques, and adding pleats, gathers, and curved shapes, you can create pockets with three-dimensional shape. This is where the real fun begins!

The goal of this chapter is to allow you to gain confidence in combining different fabrics and techniques to produce items that will hold whatever tools or supplies you need to carry. In the interest of offering complete projects, I have specified certain sizes and shapes for each, but it is my hope that once you feel comfortable with the process, you will begin to play with these aspects of the designs and modify and/or completely change them to suit your tastes.

I encourage you to use paper, muslin, or other inexpensive fabrics when testing a new design, by basting or stapling it together and determining if it forms the pocket you had in mind. Fabric can be formed into whatever you can imagine by using folds and pleats — whether you opt for utter simplicity or wild complexity is up to you.

Hanging Shoe Rack

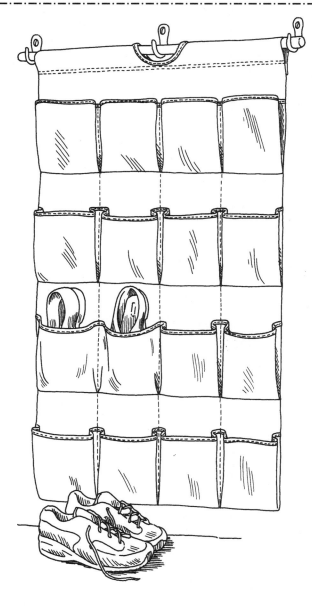

This is a basic multiple-pocket wall hanging that can be adapted for many uses, including toys, sewing or shop tools, or art supplies. Any stable woven fabric, such as burlap, can be used: The important thing is that the fabric is durable and woven loosely enough to allow air to circulate through the weave. The instructions here are for a shoe rack that will fit a men's size 9 shoe (length, 12"; girth, 10"), but most other shoes will fit in the pockets. This shoe rack holds eight pairs of shoes: large shoes fit only one shoe per pocket; small shoes fit one pair per pocket. More than one pair of smaller-sized sandals or slippers will fit into one pocket, however.

Materials

2⅔ yards fabric, at least 54" wide (4⅛ yards for
 widths as narrow as 36")
5 yards double-fold bias binding, ½" wide
One wooden dowel, 26" long x ½" diameter
Sewing thread

Cutting Layout

Following the measurements and layout shown, draw the pieces on the fabric, mark, and cut out. The pieces in this project are:

A. Front and back backing, 25" wide x 52" long

B. Pocket strips, 9" wide x 41" long

On the front backing, on the right side of the fabric, mark in chalk horizontal lines 15½", 28", and 40½" down from the top edge. Also mark vertical lines ½" in from each side edge and at 6" intervals in between. Mark the back backing with a horizontal line 3" down from the top edge.

Each of the four pockets on a pocket strip has 1" inverted pleats at both sides. Therefore, on each pocket strip, on the right side of the fabric, mark in chalk ½" seam allowance on the left edge. Then, across the strip, mark two 1" pleat lines followed by a 6" pocket span, five 1" pleat lines followed by a 6" pocket span (x 3), and two 1" pleat lines followed by ½" seam allowance, as indicated in the illustration.

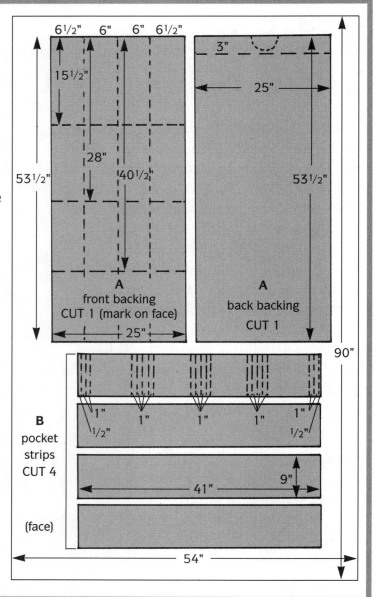

Preparing the Pockets

1 Press under ½" along one long edge of each pocket strip.

2 Bind along the opposite edge of each strip (see page 29).

3 Fold and press the pleats into each pocket strip, so that the inverted pleat folds meet at the front. The pocket span edges are pressed back to back; all other fold lines are pressed face to face.

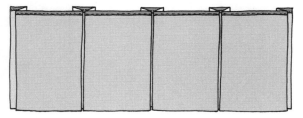

CUSTOMIZING THE SHOE RACK

You can make the Hanging Shoe Rack as indicated in these instructions, or you can customize it to fit your shoes.

In order to determine the pattern dimensions, you must first take the measurements of your shoes. Measure the average length of your shoes (**a**); and measure the distance over the width of your largest shoes at their tallest point (usually across the area where the laces tie) (**b**).

- **To determine the width of the pocket strip,** take ²/₃ of the length (**a**), and add 1" for the hem.

- **To determine the length of the pocket strip,** take (**b**), multiply it by four (four pockets across each strip) and add ¹/₂" seam allowance on either side (1" total).
- **To determine the distance between the pocket strips,** base to base (when placing on the backing), take (**a**), and add ¹/₂".
- **To determine the pocket span size,** subtract 4" from (**b**). Then, **to determine the width of the backing,** multiply the pocket span size by 4, and add a ¹/₂" seam allowance on either side (1" total).
- **To determine the length of the backing,** take (**a**), multiply it by the number of pocket strips you plan on making, add ¹/₂" for between each pocket strip, and add ¹/₂" seam allowances for the top and bottom (1" total), plus 3" at the top for the dowel casing.

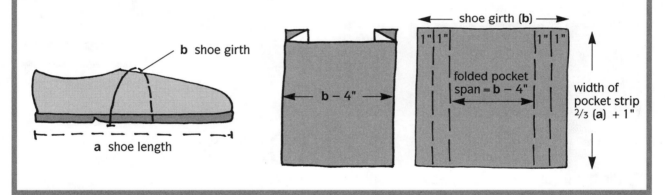

b shoe girth

a shoe length

shoe girth (**b**)

1" 1"   1" 1"

folded pocket
span = b – 4"

b – 4"

width of
pocket strip
²/₃ (a) + 1"

Attaching the Pockets

4 With the pleats pinned closed, pin the first pocket strip to the right side of the front backing piece, along the top of the 15¹/₂" horizontal line, matching the 6" pocket spans to the 6" marks on the backing. Using a ¹/₂" seam allowance, stitch along the sides. Using ¹/₈" seam allowance, stitch across the bottom of the pocket strip.

5 Repeat step 4 for the other three pocket strips, lining them up with the corresponding horizontal lines on the backing. The bottom pocket should be located ¹/₂" up from the bottom raw edge.

6 Stitch along the marked vertical lines on the shoe rack, stitching over the pocket strips and between the pocket span edges, folding these edges back as you sew. Stitch from the bottom up, to flatten the pockets as you sew. Backstitch three to four stitches at each pocket opening to reinforce the stress points.

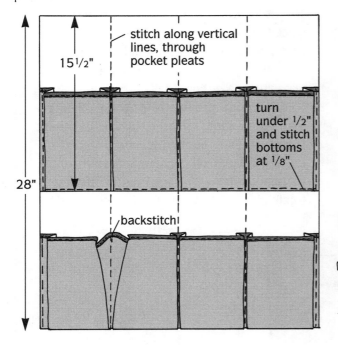

stitch along vertical lines, through pocket pleats

15½"

turn under ½" and stitch bottoms at ⅛"

28"

backstitch

7 Pin the pleats along the sides of the shoe rack inward, to get them out of the way of the outer edge of the backing. Place the unpocketed backing piece on top of the pocketed one, right sides facing. Using a ½" seam allowance, stitch the two pieces together along the sides and bottom. Use the existing pocket strip side seams as a guide, and stitch just below the bottom pocket edges along the bottom. Do not catch the pleats or pocket bottoms in these seams. Leave the top edge of the shoe rack open. Turn right-side out and press flat.

8 Restitch the seams along the pocket strip bottoms, through all layers, to reinforce the pockets, and connect the back and front backings.

Making the Dowel Casing

9 Find the center point along the top edge. Measure 3" to each side of this point and mark. Measure 2¾" down from the center point and mark. Connect these three points with a curved semicircular line. Cut out the semicircle. Bind the interior of the curve, enclosing the front and back backing inside the binding.

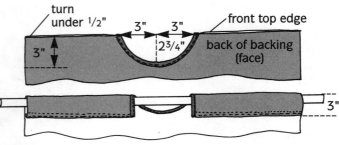

turn under ½"

3"   3"

front top edge

3"

2¾"

back of backing (face)

3"

10 Turn under and press ½" along the top edge. Fold the top edge toward the back and pin the turned under edge at the marked 3" horizontal line. Stitch the casing ⅛" from the turned edge across the full length of the top edge to make the dowel casing. Sew a second line of stitching close to the first to reinforce the casing.

11 Insert the dowel, and find a place to hang your shoe rack. You can hang it from one nail or hook placed at the center point of the dowel, or on three nails placed at the center and at both ends of the dowel, if your shoes are heavy.

Bucket Caddy

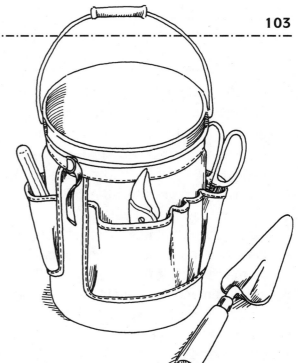

The bucket caddy is a double apron designed to hang from its strap around a 5-gallon bucket. It allows you to carry the tools you need for a garden or carpentry project on the outside of the bucket, leaving the empty bucket available to fill with materials. For light-duty use, heavy twill or canvas fabric works well. For heavy use, consider making the caddy out of nylon pack cloth or a fabric-backed vinyl. I made mine with unbleached canvas and a different color binding for each pocket. The result was a cheerful, functional item, and I used up some old binding scraps in the process.

Materials

⅔ yard fabric, 60" wide;
   or 1 yard fabric, 44" wide
2 yards cotton or nylon webbing, 1" wide
4 yards double-fold bias binding, ½" wide
Two 1" D rings
Sewing thread

Cutting Layout

Because the Bucket Caddy has two pocket bags (one on each side of the bucket), you will be making two of everything. For 60" fabric, fold selvage to selvage, right sides together. For narrower fabric, fold up an 8" strip across the width, mark and cut bag backings, then place the pocket patterns on the remaining fabric. Following the measurements and layout shown, draw the pieces on the right side of the fabric, mark, and cut out. The pieces in this project are:

A. Bag backing, 16" wide x 12" long

B. Small pocket, 6" square

C. Large pocket, start with 26" wide x 8" long piece

The large tool pockets are designed to billow out from the backing. The large pocket is a trapezoid shape, angled so that the upper edge is longer than the lower edge. It is essential that the angled sides of the pocket measure 8" (the same dimension as the height of the pocket at its center), so that the pocket, when sewn onto the backing, measures 16" wide x 8" high, all the way across the backing.

To mark this shape, draw a rectangle 26" wide x 8" high. Mark the center 6" wide pocket, leaving 10" extensions on each side. On the 16" bottom edge of the pocket mark 5" extensions on each side of the center 6" pocket. Now, draw a diagonal from the end of each 5" extension on the bottom edge to the end of each 10" extension on the top edge. Measure 8" up from the bottom of this diagonal line, and draw a curved line joining this point to the side point of the 6" wide pocket mark along the top edge on either side. The diagonal line is now correct — the pocket sides measure 8".

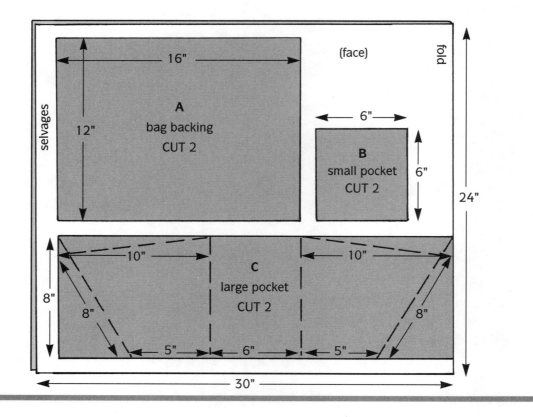

Binding and Attaching

1 Bind the top edge of the 6" x 6" pockets (see page 29).

2 Press under ¹/₂" along the sides of the two 6" pockets. Measure 5¹/₂" in from either side along the bottom edge of the large pockets, and mark these points with chalk. Pin one 6-pocket to one large pocket, so that the small pocket is positioned upside-down, 1¹/₂" from the bottom edge of the large pocket and aligned with the marks. Using ¹/₂" seam allowance, stitch the small pocket to the large pocket, along the pinned edge. Repeat with the remaining small and large pocket.

3 Flip the small pockets up and stitch the pocket sides in place, ¹/₈" in from the edges, backstitching at the pocket corners. Draw two lines on each small pocket, located 1¹/₂" in from the pocket edges. Stitch along these dividing lines to make slots for pens and small tools.

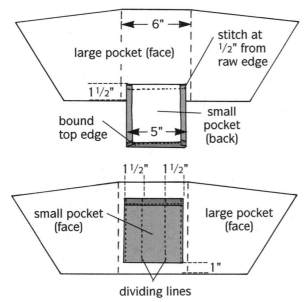

4 Bind the curved top edges of the two large pockets. Lay a large pocket onto each bag backing, with the wrong side of the

pocket facing the right side of the backing. Using a ¹/₄" seam allowance, stitch along the bottom.

5 Measure 5" in from each side edge of the bag backing and mark. Lay the center of the large pocket flat on the bag backing, and pin the center of the pocket onto the backing along these marks.

6 Using the marked lines as guidelines, stitch the pocket dividing seams to separate the center (flat) pocket from the side (billowing) pockets.

7 Line up the large pocket side edges with the backing side edges, so that the side pockets have a billow in them. With chalk, sketch rounded corners, and, using a ³/₈" seam allowance, stitch the pocket to the backing following the rounded line around each corner.

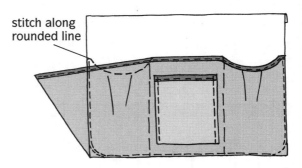

Finishing the Pocket Bags

8 Trim the bottom corners of the pocket bags along the rounded shape. To cover the seam allowances that connect the large pocket to the backing, bind around the sides and bottom of the bags, starting at the left-hand upper corner and folding under the raw binding end. Ease the binding around the curves, and turn under the raw edge of the binding at the right-hand upper corner.

9 Press ½" along the top of each pocket bag toward the face of the bag.

10 Cut a 48" length of webbing.

11 Starting 3" in from one end of the webbing, pin the webbing to the face of one of the pocket bags (covering the pressed-down edge). Stitch the webbing to the pocket bag, ⅛" in from each edge of the webbing. Leaving 2" between bags, pin the webbing to the face of the second one, and stitch ⅛" in from each edge of the webbing.

12 On the longer end of the webbing, turn under 1" twice, and sew a box stitch to finish the end.

13 Thread two **D** rings onto the 3" end of webbing. Turn under 1" twice, and pin this end to the back of the pocket bag, to make a ½" loop of webbing that holds the two **D** rings. Stitch the turned under end of webbing to the pocket bag backing with a box stitch.

DESIGN OPTIONS

✂ Change the pocket configurations to fit specific tools.

✂ Use a snap buckle instead of D rings to fasten the strap.

✂ Change the size of the pocket bags and the length of the webbing to fit around vessels other than a 5-gallon bucket. To do this, measure the circumference of the container. Decide how wide and how long to make the two pocket bags, remembering to leave a few inches in between for the strap and buckle. Try making a large caddy to fit around a 55-gallon garbage can. You can use it for yard clean-up, and, if you add some webbing loops, you can hang your rake and shovel.

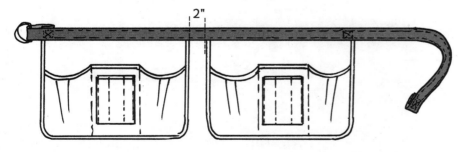

14 *To use,* wrap the caddy around the bucket, and thread the long strap through both **D** rings, and back through one **D** ring, and pull tight. (If the bucket handle interferes, lift the strap between the pocket bags up and over the handle, seating the strap in the groove just below the lip of the bucket.)

Carpenter's Half-Apron

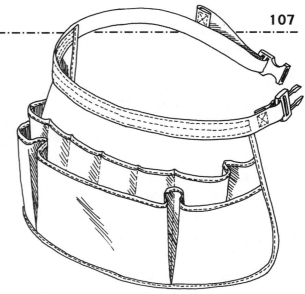

Depending on the end use you have in mind for this apron, it can be made of almost any material — leather, canvas, pack cloth, vinyl, or even calico for light duty. If used for carpentry, try making the apron and flat pocket out of canvas, and the outer pocket, which will hold heavy tools, out of leather.

Materials

½ yard fabric, at least 45" wide (1 yard, if narrower)

3 yards double-fold bias binding, ½" wide (wider, if using very thick material)

44" (or more) cotton or nylon webbing 1" wide

One snap buckle

Sewing thread

Cutting Layout

Following the measurements and layout shown, draw the pieces on the fabric, mark, and cut out.

The pieces in this project are:

A. Inner pocket strip, 21" wide x 8" long

B. Outer pocket strip, 26" wide x 7" long

C. Apron back, 12" wide, 18" long at top, 21" long at bottom

To make the apron back pattern, draw a 12" wide x 18" long rectangle. Make a mark 2" down from both top corners. On the bottom edge, extend the length of the rectangle out 1½" on either side. Connect these extensions to the bottom of the 2" marks with diagonal lines, to form the angled sides of the apron back.

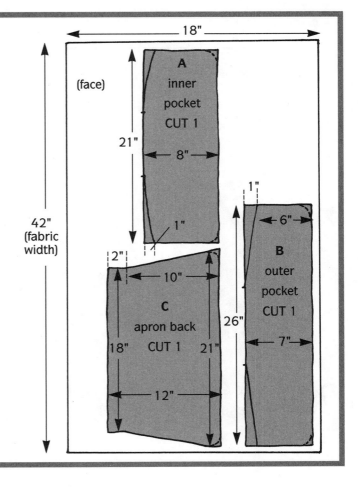

Marking Pleats and Binding Pockets

1 Find and mark the center line on the face of the outer pocket strip. Then, mark pleat lines at 4", 4½", 5", 5½", and 6" on either side of the center. Stitch along all ten pleat lines. This will help the pleats to fold naturally and will act as a sewing guide later in the project.

Fold and press the pleats, as shown below, to form two inverted pleats between the three pockets. (Two outer folds come toward the 5" placement line on each side of the pocket.)

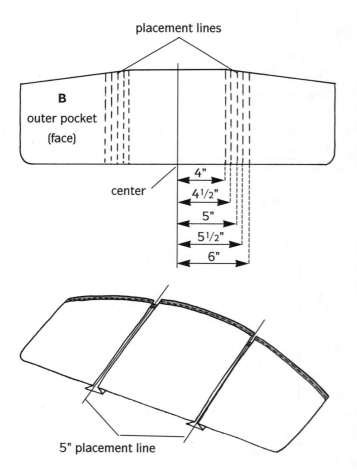

2 Bind the top edge of both the inner and outer pocket strips (see page 29).

Attaching the Nonpleated Pocket Strip

3 Mark lines in chalk on the inner pocket strip, at 3", 8½", 10½", 12½", and 18" from the left-hand side.

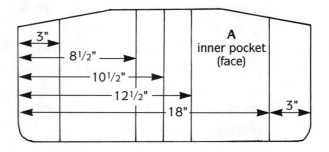

4 Place the wrong side of the inner pocket strip on top of the right side of the apron back, matching side and bottom edges. Using a ¼" seam allowance, stitch around the side and bottom edges of the pocket. The excess fabric, caused by attaching a straight piece to a tapered apron back, will form three-dimensional pockets later in the project.

5 Stitch down the five marked lines, on the inner pocket strip, to form six pockets, pushing the billow of excess fabric to the middle pockets (located between 3" and 8½" and between 12½" and 18").

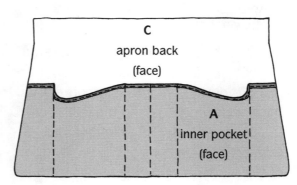

Attaching the Pleated Pocket

6 Now push the billow of the two pockets all the way toward the outer edges of the apron. Measure from the center of the pocket strip (the 10½" mark) out 4" in both directions and mark.

7 Lay the wrong side of the outer pocket strip on top of the inner pocket strip, lining up the center-stitched (5") pleat lines with the 4" marks you just made on the inner pocket strip. Being careful not to catch the pleat edges, stitch along these pleat lines, starting at the bottom edge, and continuing the seam all the way to the top edge of the inner pocket strip, thus forming two new pocket divisions on this piece, and creating a pleated pocket in the center of the outer pocket strip. Note that the two pockets created on the inner pocket strip, toward the outer edge of the apron, are three-dimensional.

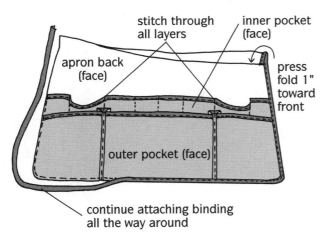

stitch through all layers

inner pocket (face)

apron back (face)

press fold 1" toward front

outer pocket (face)

continue attaching binding all the way around

8 Line up and pin the corners of the outer pocket strip to the inner pocket strip and the apron. Using a ¼" seam allowance, stitch around the side and bottom edges of the outer pocket strip.

Putting It All Together

9 Starting at one side, attach bias binding all around the sides and bottom of the apron, leaving the binding's raw edge at both top edges. Stitch around the binding close to the edge, making sure to catch the back of the binding in the seam, as you stitch over the two pleats.

10 Fold and press 1" along the top of the apron toward the front.

Attaching the Waist Belt

11 Cut a length of webbing long enough to amply fit the waist of the person who will be wearing the apron, with excess for adjustment, and an additional 3" for attaching the buckle. (I used 44" of webbing for a 30" waist.)

12 Thread one end of the webbing through one half of the snap buckle. Fold under ½", and then 1½" to form a loop. Box stitch the ½" hem securely in place.

13 Decide which side of the apron you wish to open and close, and, with the buckle and box stitch extending just beyond that apron edge, pin the webbing to the front of the apron, covering the pressed hem. Using a ⅛" seam allowance, stitch around the webbing. Box stitch at either edge of the apron.

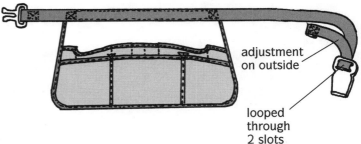

adjustment on outside

looped through 2 slots

14 Thread the other end of the webbing through the other half of the buckle, so that the adjustable strap is on the outside (for easy adjustment). Fold over 1/2", then 1" of the end of the webbing, and box stitch this hem closed. (This will also prevent the webbing from pulling through buckle end). If you prefer to use **D** rings instead of a snap buckle, follow the directions for attaching **D** rings in the Bucket Caddy project, page 106.

DESIGN OPTIONS

✂ Combine this pocket configuration with the bib apron from the Apron project page 50, for a full-bib carpenter's apron.

✂ Many carpenters hang their apron from their suspenders. For a great gift for the professional or the weekend handyman, purchase or make suspenders that match the apron.

✂ Design aprons with multiple layers of pockets. All you need to remember is that each subsequent pocket layer that you add will have to be seamed through the previous layers, which will form new pocket divisions on them. Plan accordingly, and experiment.

✂ Use your knowledge of pocket construction to create wall-hanging storage bins, or waterproof, suction-cupped bathtub toy holders, or a multitude of other handy storage items.

Traveling Jewelry Bag

This trifold case can be made with several different pocket combinations. I offer three kinds of pockets in this project, but you can customize your version depending upon your jewelry storage needs: increase or reduce the number of pockets to hold more or fewer earrings, increase the size of the zipper-secured storage, or make the whole bag larger or smaller. You can choose from a variety of woven fabrics, although heavier fabrics might not fold as well.

Materials

½ yard muslin, twill, or other woven fabric, 36" wide
7" wide x 14" long piece decorative fabric for outside face (optional)
Hook and loop fastener, 1" wide x 4" long
5" zipper
2 yards double-fold bias binding, ¼" or ½" wide
Sewing thread

Cutting Layout

The outer cover may be cut from a piece of decorative fabric, if desired. Following the measurements and layout shown, draw the pieces on the fabric, mark, and cut out. The pieces in this project are:

A. Upper inside panel, 7" wide x 6½" long, with rounded upper corners

B. Lower inside panel, 7" wide x 8½" long, with rounded bottom corners

C. Large earring pocket, 7" wide x 4½" long

D. Medium earring pocket, 7" wide x 3½" long

E. Small earring pocket, 7" wide x 2½" long

F. Patch pocket, 6" wide x 5¼" long

G. Patch pocket flap, 6" wide x 4" long

H. Outer cover, 7" wide x 14" long, with rounded corners

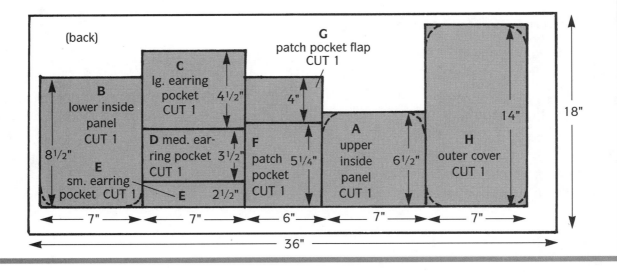

Attaching the Zipper

1 Using a ¹/₂" seam allowance, stitch the upper inside panel (**A**) to the lower inside panel (**B**) along the straight (nonrounded) edge, using normal stitch length for the first and last 1" of the stitching line, and basting stitches for the 5" in between. Backstitch at the beginning and end of both 1" normal stitching lines. Press seam open.

2 Attach the zipper along this seam (see page 34). The joined upper and lower inside panels will now be referred to as the "bag panel."

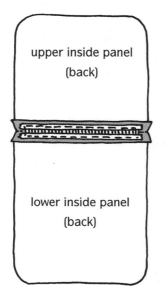

upper inside panel (back)

lower inside panel (back)

Making the Earring Pockets

3 Turn and press under ¹/₄" twice on one of the 7" edges of the large (**C**), medium (**D**), and small (**E**) earring pockets. Using ¹/₈" seam allowance, stitch these hems.

4 Place the large earring pocket (**C**) wrong side down on the lower half of the bag panel face, lining up the bottom and side

edges. Place the medium earring pocket (**D**) on top of the large earring pocket, and the small earring pocket (**E**) on top of the medium one. Line up the bottom and side edges of all four pieces, and sketch rounded corners on the top layer. Carefully trim both corners so that they are rounded. Using ¹/₄" seam allowance, stitch the sides and bottom edges of all three pockets.

5 Using chalk, mark vertical lines down the pocket faces at 2", 3¹/₂", and 5" in from the left-hand edge of the bag panel. Stitch along these divider lines through all four layers, backstitching at the top of the largest earring pocket.

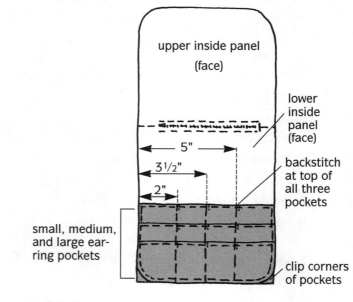

upper inside panel (face)

lower inside panel (face)

5"

3¹/₂"

2"

backstitch at top of all three pockets

small, medium, and large earring pockets

clip corners of pockets

Making the Patch Pocket

6 Turn under and press ¹/₂" on three sides of the patch pocket (**F**). Turn under and press ¹/₄", then ¹/₂" on the remaining 6" edge, creating the top edge hem. Stitch the hem at ³/₈" in from the top edge.

7 Pin the hook side of the fastener to the face of the patch pocket (**F**), centered along the hem edge and ⅛" down from the edge. Stitch around all edges of the hook to secure to the pocket.

hook strip — / hem
(face) patch pocket
turn under ½" all around

8 Pin the loop side of the fastener to the face of the patch pocket flap (**G**), ½" up from the bottom edge and centered. Fold the flap in half, right sides together. Sketch rounded corners along the bottom edge, and, using ½" seam allowance, stitch the flap together, following the rounded corners, and leaving a 2" opening at the center. Clip the corners to eliminate bulk, and turn the flap right-side out.

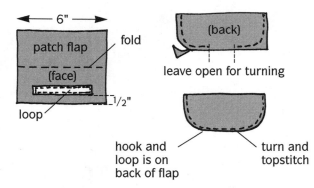

6"
patch flap   fold
(face)
loop   ½"
(back)
leave open for turning
hook and loop is on back of flap
turn and topstitch

9 Turn the raw edges of the opening in, and slipstitch the opening closed. Topstitch, ⅛" in from the edges, around the entire flap.

10 Pin the patch pocket to the bag panel, ½" above the zipper and centered. Using ⅛" seam allowance, stitch around the sides and bottom of the pocket to secure to the bag.

11 Attach the pocket flap to the pocket by lining up and fastening the two sides of the hook and loop. Using ⅛" seam allowance, stitch along the top of the pocket flap to secure to the bag.

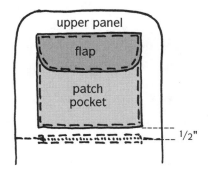

upper panel
flap
patch pocket
½"

Attaching the Outer Cover

12 Pin the bag panel to the outer cover (**H**), wrong sides facing. Trim the lower corners of the bag panel to match the rounded curves of the outer cover. Using ¼" seam allowance, stitch the two pieces together.

13 To form the bottom of the zipper pocket, stitch a straight line across the jewelry bag, above the top of the earring pockets, through all thicknesses, being careful not to catch the earring pockets in the seam.

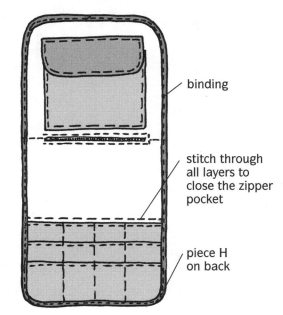

binding
stitch through all layers to close the zipper pocket
piece H on back

14 Bind the entire bag (see page 29).

15 Cut a 24" piece of binding. Turn under the ends, and stitch along the length of binding, to make a clean-finished tie for the bag. (You can also use grosgrain ribbon, hemmed at either end.) On the outer cover, center the tie on the top edge of the bag and pin. Stitch the tie to the bag along the binding seam, with 16" of tie extending down the length of the bag, and the remaining 8" extending above the top edge.

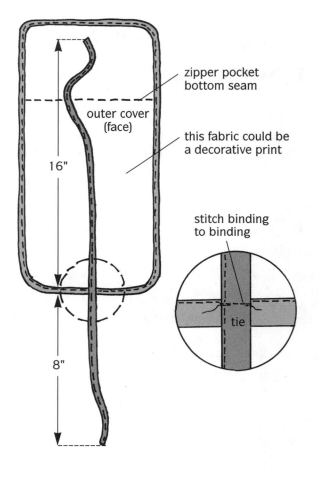

zipper pocket
bottom seam

outer cover
(face)

this fabric could be
a decorative print

16"

stitch binding
to binding

tie

8"

DESIGN OPTIONS

✂ Add a large flap over the earring pockets to prevent any earrings from falling out. The stitching line that attaches this flap will also form the bottom of the zipper pocket.

✂ Change the flap (upper) pocket to a different pocket configuration to better suit your personal jewelry collection.

✂ Make small loops out of ribbon or binding, and stitch one end to the bag. Sew the stud end of a small snap onto the other end of the ribbon. Sew the socket end of the snap to the bag. Rings can then be threaded through the loops and snapped into place.

✂ Make loops along the outside of the zipper pocket to string bracelets or watches around.

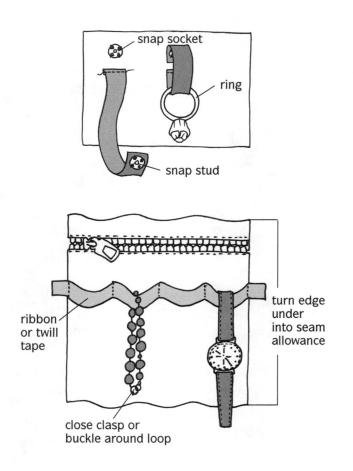

snap socket

ring

snap stud

ribbon
or twill
tape

turn edge
under
into seam
allowance

close clasp or
buckle around loop

seven

Padded Practicality: More than Just Pillows

- *Padded Shoulder Strap*
- *Padded Handle Cover*
- *Hinged Stadium Seat*
- *Mattress Pad or Cushion Cover*
- *Insulated Lunch Bag*

Padding adds a new dimension to sewn products. The addition of foam, batting, and other soft fillers can add comfort and insulation to your projects. Interfacing or buckram can be used to stiffen a section of a project. The textures of these paddings varies: dense foam feels very different than polyester batting. If you go to a store and look at padded items, you will note that there is amazing variation in both the design and the fillings used to construct them.

The projects in this chapter all use multiple layers of fabric to fully cover a padded layer. Once you know how to sew the basic constructions (which are really just variations on what you have already learned), you can customize, modify, and change shapes and fillings to create an endless array of padded items, both functional and decorative.

Padded Shoulder Strap

This strap can be fastened to a soft-sided briefcase, luggage pieces, or tool buckets to help make carrying your load more comfortable. It can be purely functional or color-coordinated to match your briefcase or luggage. Any item that has holes, loops, or D rings can be fastened onto the spring hooks of this strap, making it a versatile addition to your luggage accessories

Materials

Heavy canvas, twill, or upholstery-weight fabric, 10" wide x 28" long
40" strap webbing or heavy twill tape, 1" wide
Two 1" snap hooks
Two 1" slider buckles
Batting or thin foam, 4" wide x 27" long
Sewing thread

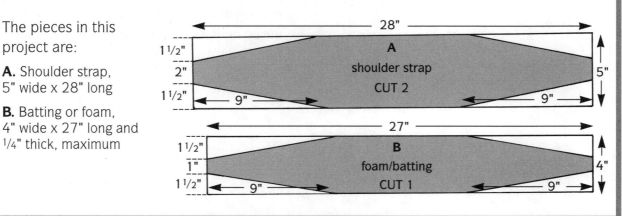

Cutting Layout

Fold fabric lengthwise, right sides together, to create a 5" wide doubled area of cloth. Following the measurements and layout shown, draw the pieces on the fabric, mark, and cut out.

The pieces in this project are:

A. Shoulder strap, 5" wide x 28" long

B. Batting or foam, 4" wide x 27" long and 1/4" thick, maximum

To taper the pattern pieces, measure the full rectangles on the strap fabric and batting. Measure 9" from each end as shown, and mark. Then measure 1 1/2" from the top and bottom on each side, mark, and connect these points to the 9" marks.

A. shoulder strap, CUT 2 — 28", 5", 1 1/2", 2", 1 1/2", 9", 9"

B. foam/batting, CUT 1 — 27", 4", 1 1/2", 1", 1 1/2", 9", 9"

Threading the Buckle and Hook Configurations

1 Cut the 40" piece of webbing in half. Pull one end of one 20" piece of webbing around the center post of the slider buckle. Turn under 1/2" hem and box stitch it in place. The hem should be snug up against the buckle; you may need to use your zipper foot.

2 Thread the end of the webbing through the snap hook, and up under the buckle, over the center post and under the other side of the buckle. Pull the webbing through so that several inches are free. This end will be stitched into the shoulder strap.

3 Repeat steps 1 and 2 with the other 20" piece of webbing, slider buckle, and snap hook.

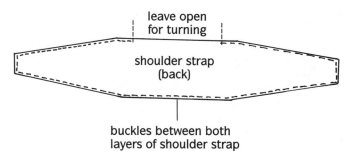

BACK VIEW

stitch around center post of buckle

Attaching the Buckle Straps to the Shoulder Strap

4 Place the strap assemblies on the face side of one shoulder strap, raw ends centered on the 2" ends of the fabric. Pin the end of the webbing to the fabric, close to the snap hook, to prevent it from getting caught in the seam line. Using a 1/4" seam allowance, stitch the webbing ends to the ends of the shoulder strap.

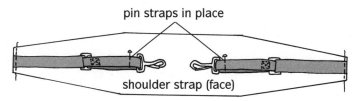

pin straps in place

shoulder strap (face)

5 Pin the two shoulder strap pieces together, right sides facing. Using 1/2" seam allowance, stitch around all edges, leaving the seam open along one of the straight sides, and backstitching at both ends.

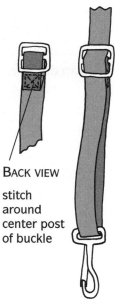

leave open for turning

shoulder strap (back)

buckles between both layers of shoulder strap

Padding the Strap

6 Clip the curves and the corners of the shoulder strap. Turn right-side out by first removing the pins holding the webbing ends down, and then pulling the webbing pieces through the opening. Press the shoulder strap flat, carefully lining up the unsewn edges so they are turned under 1/2" and are flush with the sewn seams.

7 Using a metal ruler or pencil, push the batting or foam into the ends of the "pillow," and adjust into place. Topstitch 1/8" from the edge, around the entire shoulder strap, pushing the padding out of the way if necessary, and carefully closing the open seam. This operation closes the seam, holds the foam in place, and reinforces the webbing attachment.

Making It Hang Right

These steps will encourage the strap to fold over your shoulder and drape properly.

8 In chalk, mark 9" in from each fabric end, and then 4" in from those marks.

9 Stitch across the shoulder strap, through all thicknesses, along these marks.

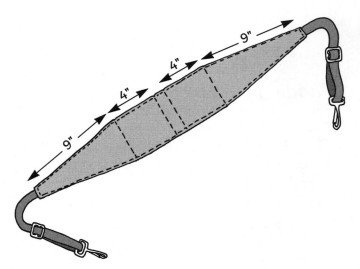

10 *To use,* hook the snap hooks to any D ring or looped bag, and try out your new comfortable carrying strap!

DESIGN OPTION: INSTRUMENT STRAP

Many musicians use shoulder and neck straps, which connect to their instruments in different ways. You can customize a strap for musician friends by choosing material in the colors they love, and adjusting the pattern to match their height and padding preferences. If the finding that connects the strap to the instrument is unusual and hard to locate, get an old strap from your friend and reuse the finding in your new strap design.

Padded Handle Cover

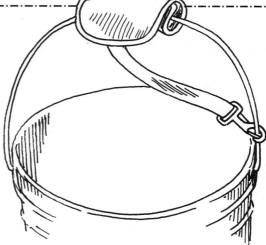

For anyone who has nearly cut off the circulation in their hands when carrying a heavy bucket or bag with hard or sharp handles, this simple padded handle cover is a blessing. The construction would work well for hanging items from your bicycle bar or a shower curtain rod, too. For this project, each side of the cover can be a different fabric. I used suede and heavy twill for mine. You can also use store-bought suede elbow patches that come in rectangular shapes with rounded corners. The optional strap and hook attachment allows you to fasten the handle cover to a piece of luggage or a bucket, so that it will be hanging there when you need it.

Materials

10" wide x 6" long piece fabric (canvas, pack cloth, or leather)

½ yard double-fold bias binding, ½" wide

5" wide x 6" long piece $\frac{3}{16}$" thick craft foam, or flat batting, or several layers of flannel

4" hook and loop fastener, ½", ¾", or 1" wide

12" nylon strap webbing, 1" wide (optional)

One snap hook (optional)

Sewing thread

Cutting Layout

Cut the 10 x 6" fabric into two 5 x 6" rectangles. Round the corners to make two of piece **A**. Following the measurements and layout shown, draw the pieces on the fabric and cut out.

The pieces in this project are:

A. Handle cover front and back, 5" wide x 6" long

B. Foam or batting, 4" wide x 5" long

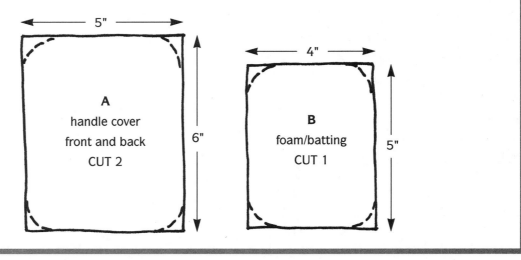

5"

A
handle cover
front and back
CUT 2

6"

4"

B
foam/batting
CUT 1

5"

Attaching the Hook and Loop

1 Attach the hook side of the fastener to the face side of one of the cover pieces, 3/4" down from the top edge (see page 36).

2 Attach the loop side of the fastener to the face side of the other cover piece, 3/4" up from the bottom edge.

Assembling the Cover

3 With wrong sides facing, pin the two cover pieces together, so that the hook and loop are at opposite ends, with the foam sandwiched between them.

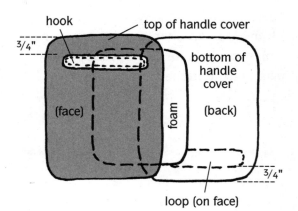

hook   top of handle cover

3/4"

bottom of handle cover

(face)   foam   (back)

3/4"

loop (on face)

4 To add the optional strap and snap hook attachment, pin one end of the webbing against the 6" edge of the cover piece face, 2" from the top, so that you will catch it in the seam (step 5). Thread the other end of the strap through the snap hook, turn under 1" at the end for a hem, and pull 1 1/2" more through the hook to form a loop. Box stitch the hem down. Pin the webbing down to the cover, so that it will not catch in any other edge seams.

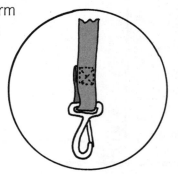

5 Using 1/4" seam allowance, stitch around the cover pieces, catching the strap in one side only, and keeping the foam centered and away from the seam lines.

6 Trim the raw edge to 1/4" (if you want to use narrower bias binding, trim the raw edge to 1/8"). Bind the periphery of the padded piece (see page 29).

7 *To use,* hang the handle cover from your suitcase or bucket, and wrap the handle whenever the load is too heavy for your hands.

CUSTOMIZING DIFFERENT-SIZED HANDLE COVERS

If you are making a handle cover for wider or larger handles, you will need to increase the length of this pattern. The distance from the bottom of the top piece of hook and loop, to the top of the bottom piece of hook and loop (**x**) is the circumference around the handles you are trying to cover (add 1" for good measure). To determine the length of the handle cover front and back pattern piece, take (**x**), add 1", and add 1 1/2" more. The foam padding should be cut 1" smaller than the handle cover pieces, so that you can attach the binding without catching the edges of the padding.

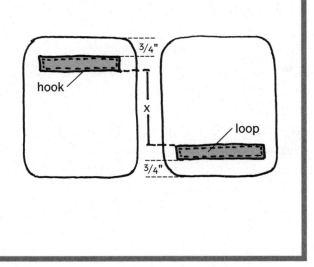

Hinged Stadium Seat

This project describes a basic method for covering a thin (1" to 2") foam pad, using welting along the edges as an abrasion-resistant seam finish. Bring the Hinged Stadium Seat on camping trips, to sports events, picnics, or wherever you think the seating might be hard. Once you know this basic technique, you can custom-fit cushions for all the unpleasantly hard chairs in your house.

Materials

1½ yards (minimum) fabric, 54" wide (nylon pack cloth or other water-repellent goods)

5 yards welting cord, ³⁄₁₆" diameter

3 yards strap webbing or heavy twill tape, 1" wide

Two 18 x 18" foam cushions, 1" to 2" thick

Seam sealer (optional)

Sewing thread

Cutting Layout

Fold the fabric in half, selvage to selvage, right sides together. Following the measurements and layout shown, draw the pieces on the fabric, mark, and cut out.

The pieces in this project are:

A. Seat front, 19 x 19"

B. Seat back, 19 x 19"

C. Welting strips, 1 1/2" wide x 5 yards long

Note: The cutting layout shows welting strips cut on the grain, to save fabric. If your fabric pattern would look better cut on the bias (diagonal), buy at least 1/2 yard extra, and follow the instructions for making a continuous bias binding strip (see page 28).

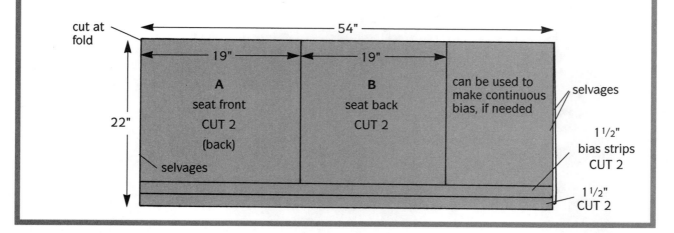

Making and Attaching the Welting

1 Cut the bias strip and the welting cord in half, making four 2½-yard lengths. Fold one of the bias strips in half over one of the welting cords. Stitch the bias strips within ⅛" of the cord, leaving the first and last 6" of the tape and cord unsewn. Trim the raw edges of the welting to ½".

2 With the raw edges lined up, pin the welting to the right side of the seat front, starting at the center of one side. Using a ½" seam allowance, carefully stitch the welting to the seat front. As you approach the end of one side, slow down so that you can stop exactly at the corner. Clip the seam allowance of the welting so it can curve around the corner. In the same manner, continue to pivot and stitch the welting around the corner. Repeat this process for remaining three corners. Stop 6" from the starting point, and backstitch.

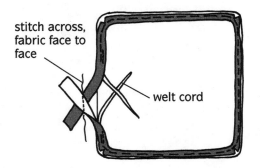

stitch across, fabric face to face

welt cord

3 To make a continuous trim, lay the two loose ends of welting next to each other over the unsewn edge of the seat front. Using chalk, mark both pieces at the spot where they would logically join. Unstitch the welting cord several inches beyond these marks. With right sides together, lay the bias strips at right

angles to each other with the chalk marks lined up. Stitch a diagonal line across them (mitered seam), and then trim the excess bias fabric. Trim the cord so that the ends meet in a different spot than the bias strip join seam. Fold the bias strip over the cord and begin sewing where you left off, backstitching to start, and ending at the point where you began attaching the welting.

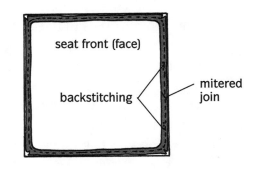

seat front (face)

backstitching

mitered join

4 Repeat steps 1 through 3 for the second seat front.

Making the Handle Hinges

5 Measure 5" in from the sides of each unwelted cushion cover (seat back), and on the face of the fabric draw lines in chalk that run the length of the pieces. Starting in the center of one of the welted cushion covers, pin the strap webbing just inside these lines, leaving a 13" handle at each outer edge and a 3" "hinge" between the two cushions. Turn under 1" of the strap webbing at one end, and overlap at the starting point.

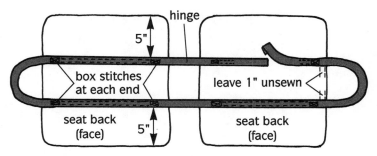

hinge

5"

box stitches at each end

leave 1" unsewn

seat back (face)

5"

seat back (face)

6 Stitch the strap webbing to the seat backs, ⅛" in from both edges of the webbing, starting and ending your stitching 1" in from the cushion edges. Box stitch the strap to the cushion at each point where the strap exits the cushion fabric and at the strap overlap seam.

Finishing the Cushions

7 Pin the handle loops down to the webbing, to prevent them from getting caught in the cushion join seam.

8 Ties can be made of cord, ribbon, or tubes of fabric stitched and turned right-side out. There will be four ties, each 8" long, sandwiched between the cushion covers and located 4" to 6" down from the top of the cushions (the ends with handles). Pin the ties to the seat backs, facing toward the right sides of the cushions.

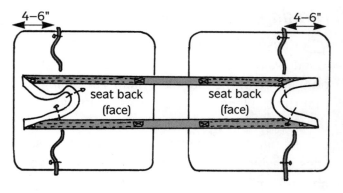

9 With right sides together, pin the seat fronts to the seat backs. With the welt seam line facing up, stitch around each cushion cover, beginning at the outer edge of the strap webbing on one side and ending at

the outer edge of the strap webbing on the other side. Stitch inside and as close to the welting seam line as you can, pivoting around the corners carefully. Turn the cushion covers right-side out.

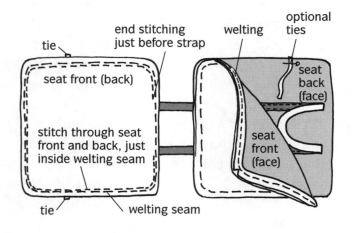

10 Bend the foam cushions in half or in thirds so that you can push them into the openings between the strap webbing. Massage the cushion covers and the foam until everything lies flat. In my experience, if you can fit the unrounded corners of the foam into the rounded fabric cushion, you'll have nice firm corners. However, if necessary, you can round the corners of the foam.

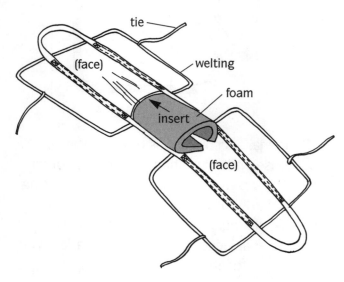

11 Turn in the seam allowance at the openings, and stitch along the inside edge of the welting seam close to the cushions; start and end the seam 1/2" beyond the actual opening. Stitch with the seat-front side up (side without straps). Pull the other half of the seat cushion back and away from the seam so the strap hinges do not get caught in the seam. Stitch *only* through the cushion covers and welting seam allowance.

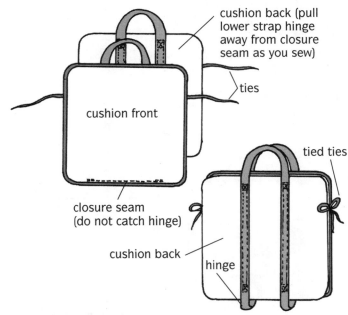

cushion back (pull lower strap hinge away from closure seam as you sew)

ties

cushion front

tied ties

closure seam
(do not catch hinge)

cushion back

hinge

DESIGN OPTIONS

✂ For a waterproof finish, seal the cushion seams with store-bought seam sealer.

✂ If you have used an airtight fabric, you might want to put some grommets in the fabric to allow air to escape. Before attaching the unwelted cushion covers to the welted ones, place the grommets in both unwelted covers, either at the corners or along one or two edges, making sure that they are well inside the seam allowance.

✂ Ties or snap buckles on loops of webbing can be inserted into the sides of the cushion covers before sewing them together, so that the hinged seat will fasten flat when not in use.

DESIGN VARIATION: MODIFIED HINGE

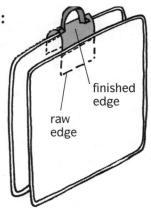

finished edge

raw edge

See the materials list and cutting layout in the main project text. In addition, you'll need a 12" piece of strap webbing, 1" wide; and two 7 x 7" squares of fabric.

Instead of making strap handles, you can make a fabric hinge between the cushions, with the handle attached to the hinge.

1 With right sides together, sew the two 7" pieces along two opposite sides and turn right-side out. Topstitch 1/8" from sewn edges. This is the hinge.

2 To make a handle, turn under 1" at both ends of the webbing. Box stitch to the hinge piece, parallel to the raw edges.

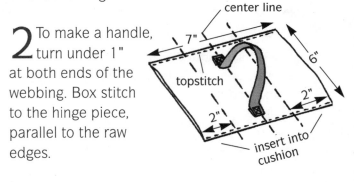

center line

7"

6"

topstitch

2"

2"

2"

insert into cushion

3 Attach welting to the cushion covers.

4 Stitch the front cushions to the back cushions, leaving a 6" opening for turning. Center the 6" openings along the edges of the cushions you want to form the hinge. Turn right-side out.

5 Insert 2" of each end of the hinge into each 6" opening, leaving 3" of the hinge exposed (the handle should be evenly spaced between the cushions). Stitch closed along the cushion edge, catching the welting, cushion cover, and hinge in the stitching. Restitch to reinforce.

Mattress Pad or Cushion Cover

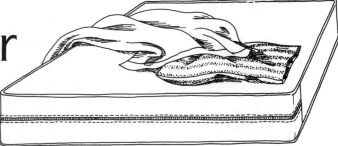

This project describes the basic method used to make a zippered cover for a foam cushion. I have based the measurements on a 36 x 80" foam pad, but you can adapt the instructions for any size cushion. You can use any fabric durable enough to hold a zipper; I recommend using something washable and breathable. Upholstery fabrics work well. I have also made these covers using a quilted mattress pad as the fabric, for indoor sleeping mattresses.

This is the same method used in professional upholstery. Use it for round or oval cushions or anything you like — you just need to determine the zipper length and cut the side panels so that they are long enough to form the zipper pockets.

Materials

5 yards fabric, at least 54" wide (7 yards, if 36" wide)
13½ yards welting cord
44" zipper
36 x 80" foam pad
Sewing thread

Cutting Layout

Following the measurements and layout shown, draw the pieces on the fabric, mark, and cut out.

The pieces in this project are:

A. Cushion covers, 37" wide x 81" long

B. Side panels, 5" wide x 81" long, CUT 2

C. End panel, 5" wide x 37" long, CUT 1

D. Zipper panels, 3" wide x 45" long, CUT 2

E. Bias strips, 1 1/2" wide x 13 1/4 yards long

Unless you are using napped, striped, or plaid fabric, you can simply cut 1 1/2" strips along the length of the fabric and miter join them to obtain the desired length (see page 29).

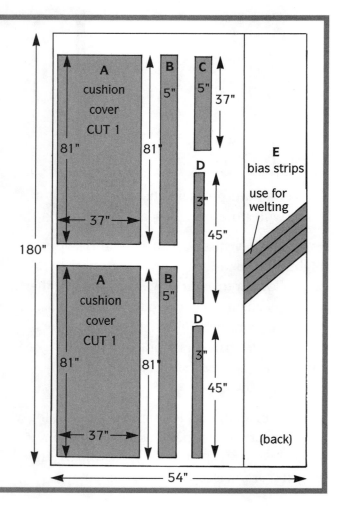

Welting the Cushion Cover

1 Sew the fabric bias strips together to make two long strips at least 6¾ yards each. Cover the welting cord with the fabric strips, leaving 6" unsewn at each end. Trim the raw edges of the welting to ½".

2 With raw edges aligned, using a ½" seam allowance, stitch the welting around the periphery of both cushion covers, and join the welting ends (see page 31).

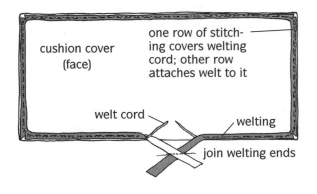

cushion cover (face)

one row of stitching covers welting cord; other row attaches welt to it

welt cord

welting

join welting ends

Making the Zipper Strip

3 Using ½" seam allowance, machine baste the zipper panels, right sides together, along their length. Press the seam open. Attach the zipper along this seam (see page 34), using a zipper foot. Open the basted seam.

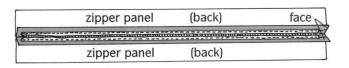

| zipper panel | (back) | face |
| zipper panel | (back) | |

4 Using ½" seam allowance, stitch the side panels to each end of the end panel, right sides together.

ABOUT CONTINUOUS ZIPPERS

When you buy zipper by the yard, and separate zipper pulls, please be aware that there is a right and a wrong way to attach the pull. If installed incorrectly, the zipper will open, but will not close. The pointed end of the zipper pull (glide) must point in the same direction as the ball end of the zipper stock. Look at both sides of the zipper teeth: one side has a ball, the other has a cup. Slide the zipper pull, with the pointed end up, onto the zipper with the ball ends up.

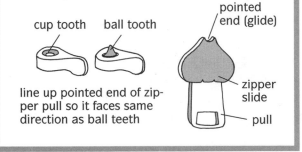

cup tooth   ball tooth

pointed end (glide)

zipper slide

pull

line up pointed end of zipper pull so it faces same direction as ball teeth

5 Using ½" seam allowance, stitch the other ends of the side panels to each end of the zipper panel, right sides together.

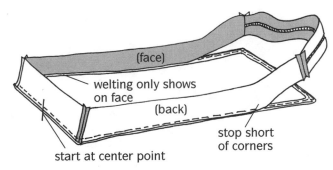

(face)

welting only shows on face

(back)

stop short of corners

start at center point

6 Mark the center point along the 36" ends of both cushion covers. Mark the center point of both the zipper panel and the end panel.

7 With right sides facing, using ½" seam allowance, start at the center point, and stitch one half of the end panel to one of the cushion covers (the seam joining the end and side panels should line up with the corner of the cushion cover). Continue stitching around one side panel, stopping 8" from the side/ zipper panel join seam. Backstitch. Repeat this step from the center point of the end panel around the other side panel.

8 Match the zipper panel center mark to the center of the cushion pad. Starting at this point, using ½" seam allowance, stitch the zipper panel to the cushion cover, continuing around the corner. Fold the side panel extension toward the inside (face) so that it forms a loop of fabric over the end of the zipper. Stitching through all layers, continue stitching along the side panel/cushion cover seam until you reach and overlap the backstitched side panel seam, to close the seam completely. Repeat this step from the center point of the zipper panel around the other side panel.

9 Repeat steps 7 and 8 for the other cushion cover. Unzip and turn the mattress cover right-side out. Insert the foam pad, and massage the fabric into place. Zip up the cover and conceal the zipper pull under the fabric pocket.

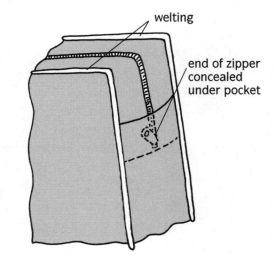

welting

end of zipper concealed under pocket

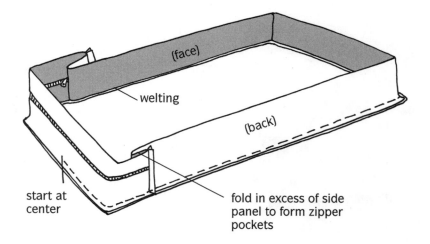

(face)

welting

(back)

start at center

fold in excess of side panel to form zipper pockets

CUSTOMIZING CUSHIONS TO FIT ANY PAD

To determine the pattern size for any cushion cover, measure the foam's length (**a**), width (**b**), and thickness (**c**), and determine zipper length (**d**).

Cushion cover size equals **a** x **b** plus ¹/₂" seam allowance for each side; in this case,

cushion cover size = **a** + 1" x **b** + 1"

The zipper should extend along one full side of the cushion (**a** or **b**) and several inches around the adjoining corners. The **zipper panel length** equals **d** plus ¹/₂" on each end; in this case,

zipper panel length = **d** + 1"

The **zipper panel width** equals ¹/₂ **c** plus ¹/₂" seam allowance for the zipper seam plus ¹/₂" seam allowance for the welt seam; in this case,

zipper panel width = ¹/₂ **c** + 1"

Zipper panel size = (**d** + 1") x (¹/₂ **c** + 1")

The **side and end panel length** equals the remaining circumference (2**a** + 2**b** − **d**) plus at least 4" for the zipper pockets (2" each end) plus ¹/₂" seam allowance at each end.

Side and end panel width equals **c** plus ¹/₂" seam allowance on each side.

Note: In this pattern, I divide the side and end panel length into thirds, placing seam at the corners, because cutting a 200" long panel is not possible. At each additional seam/join, I add a ¹/₂" seam allowance.

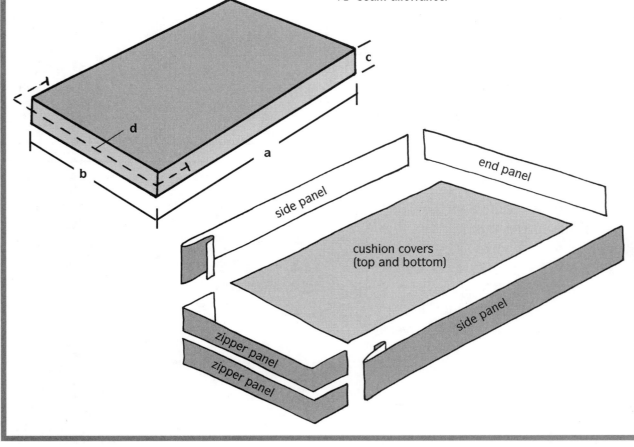

Insulated Lunch Bag

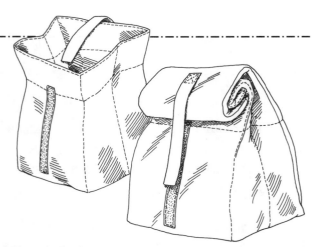

Take this fashionable, functional lunch bag to work or play. This bag holds a canned drink, sandwich, fruit, and candy bar comfortably. Use waterproof fabric for the inside and the bottom of this bag, and make the outer shell from any washable, durable fabric. The instructions here are for a lunch bag 5" wide x 7" long x 12" high.

Materials

½ yard waterproof fabric, at least 36" wide
½ yard fabric for outer shell, at least 36" wide
1½ yards single-fold bias binding, ½" wide
6" hook and loop fastener, at least 1" wide
¼ yard foam or batting, at least 30" wide
  and ¼" thick
Sewing thread

Cutting Layout

Following the measurements and layout shown, draw pieces on the fabric, mark, and cut out.

The pieces in this project are:

A. Bag side panel, 25" wide x 13" long

B. Bag bottom, 8" wide x 6" long

C. Side panel foam, 24" wide x 8" long

D. Bottom foam, 5" wide x 7" long

In chalk on the face of the bag side panel, mark vertical lines at the ½" seam allowances, and at 2½", 2½", 7", 2½", 2½", and 7" across the piece. Mark a horizontal line 4½" down from the top raw edge. In chalk on the face of one bag bottom piece, mark ½" seam allowances, which will form a 5" x 7" rectangle in the center of the piece.

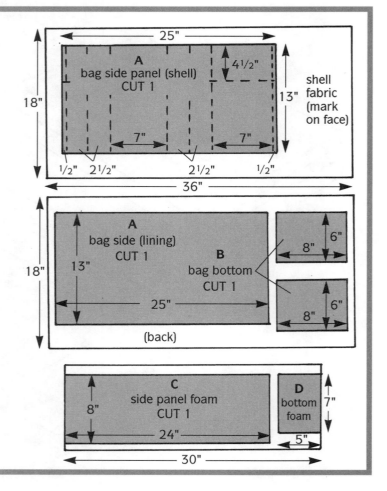

Insulating and Quilting the Bag Sides

1 With right sides facing, using 1/2" seam allowance, stitch the two bag side pieces (liner and shell) together, along the top edge. Press open and fold back over itself to form the finished top edge. Topstitch 1/4" from the top edge.

2 Pin the side panel foam piece between these two layers 1/2" up from the bottom edge, centered between the side seam allowances. Stitch from the top edge down along the vertical chalk lines (but not the two seam allowance lines). Stitch along the horizontal 4" chalk line, pulling the two fabrics taut to prevent tucks from forming.

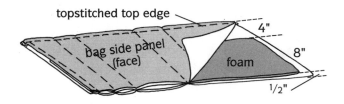

3 Hand or machine baste the side and bottom seam allowances of the two side panel pieces, to prevent them from being pulled by the foam.

Hook and Loop Fasteners

4 Pin the edge of the hook side of the fastener centered in one of the 7" wide panels (of the side panel), hook side facing down, 1" below the horizontal stitch line, and extending up toward the top edge of the panel. Box stitch the 1" piece that is below the stitch line, leaving a 5" hook tab above the stitch line unsewn; this will secure the loop fastener.

5 Pin the loop side of the fastener to the other 7" panel, loop side facing out, centered just below the horizontal stitch line, and extending down toward the bottom of the bag. Stitch around the entire piece of loop.

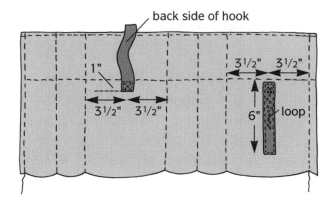

Attaching the Bag Bottom and Sides

6 Pin the bottom foam between the two bag bottom fabric pieces, with the wrong side of the fabric facing the foam. Stitch along the 1/2 seam allowance, encasing the foam.

7 Pin the bottom bag piece to the shell side of the raw (bottom) edge side panel, with the 5" side lined up with the 5" panel next to the seam allowance. Using 1/2" seam allowance, stitch the bag bottom to the side panel, pivoting and turning when you reach each corner.

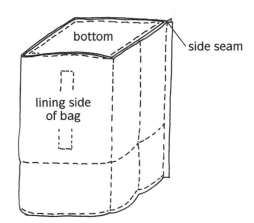

8 Line up the seam allowances of the side panel, and, using ¹/₂" seam allowance, stitch the side seam, starting at the bottom corner where the seam allowances meet. Make sure that the top edges are flush.

Binding Inside Seams

9 Trim all seam allowances to ³/₈". If there is any foam exposed in the seam allowances, trim it out to eliminate bulk. On one end of the bias binding, with right sides together, stitch across the binding ¹/₄" from the end. Turn and press right-side out. Place this finished end of bias binding at the top corner of the side seam, and sew through both sides of binding to conceal the seam allowance (see page 29).

10 Continue binding around the bottom join seam, turning under the final edge of the bias binding for a clean finish.

Turn the bag right-side out, and press the stitched fold lines to "train" them to fold accordion-style. Fill the bag, roll down the top, and close using the hook and loop.

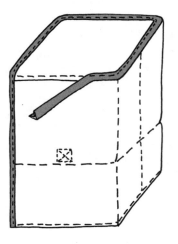

PRACTICAL CONSIDERATIONS

Padded bags are complex in the sense that they must be lined, so that the padding is covered on both sides. Figuring out how to make everything fit, which is determined by the thickness of the padding, can be tricky. In this project, the padding is thin enough that we did not have to compensate for thickness by adding extra fabric. For thicker padding, the shell has to be cut larger than the liner to allow room for the extra padding. This is similar to the difference in construction between the Hinged Stadium Seat (see page 122), which has no side panels, and the Mattress Pad or Cushion Cover (see page 126), which has panels to accommodate the width of the foam.

The other difficulty encountered when making padded constructions is finding a way to anchor the padding so that it does not shift inside the fabric shell. In this project, vertical and horizontal stitch lines were used but they had to be sewn while the side panels were flat, since the bag is too small, once closed, to fit around the sewing machine arm. For larger bags, these anchoring lines can be done after the bag is constructed. A completed inner bag (with bottom already attached) can be slipped inside an outer bag (with bottom attached). The padding can be placed in between, and the only raw edges left would be along the top, which can then easily be finished with binding. The padding is anchored by stitching along the side seams, or by using decorative stitching, such as quilting, sewn through all layers of the finished bag.

Customized Patterns and Technical Design

eight

- *Tool Tote*
- *Summertime Bedroll*
- *Dog Bed*
- *Saw Blade Holder*
- *Accordion File*

Developing Designs

When I set out to design a new item, I sketch it several times first, to address both the design and the techniques involved to complete the design. Design issues include the aesthetics of the piece as well as practical considerations such as:

✂ What functions should this item serve?

✂ Are certain fabrics best suited to this end use?

✂ Does this item need to fit certain contents or fit in specific spaces? How large or small?

✂ How should it open and close?

✂ Should the pockets face a particular direction or be a certain shape?

✂ How will the raw edges be finished?

✂ In what order should it be sewn?

Technique issues address whether an item can be sewn easily, how to use fabric most efficiently, and other specific concerns (e.g., In what order should the steps be done? Through which layers should fasteners be sewn? Are there stress points? Where is reinforcement stitching needed?).

I often cut paper shapes and fold them various ways to see what might work. My first attempt with fabric is usually a ragged mess by the time I have stitched, torn out, restitched, and reshaped the various elements. The patterns offered in this book have been through my technical design process, but you may find other details to add or modify as you sew. Throughout the projects, I have tried to include some ideas of why and how I devised particular details a certain way. If you want to change any details to better suit your practical or aesthetic needs, I advise you to first work with paper and muslin pattern pieces until you have worked out the "bugs," and then proceed to finer fabrics.

Modifying Patterns

The dimensions and details I have chosen for the projects are not sacred! You can play with the sizes, shapes, trims, and findings; however, to do so, you will need to alter certain things (e.g., seam allowances). Chapters 2 and 3 clarify many of the technical details you will need to address when modifying patterns. Here are some common ones.

✂ Any time you change a binding width, you need to consider changing the corresponding seam allowance, or your finished piece will become visually larger or smaller than planned.

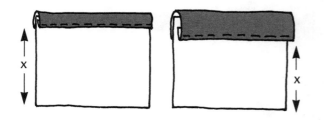

✂ If you remove binding and add a hem instead, you'll need to add additional seam allowance for the hem.

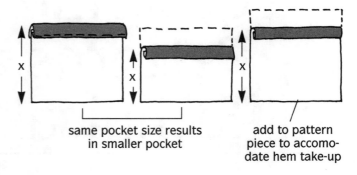

same pocket size results in smaller pocket

add to pattern piece to accomodate hem take-up

✂ Pocket sizes must be changed if you decide to use a pleated instead of a flat pocket.

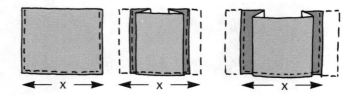

✂ If a pocket has a zipper and you'd rather use snaps, think through the process on paper. The zipper pattern has ½-inch seam allowances built in; you'll need to change that to a hemmed or bound pocket and a flap long enough to overlap and snap. Redesign the pattern pieces accordingly. Try it out in muslin, using pen markings instead of real snaps. Then move on to the real fabric, using your modified pattern dimensions.

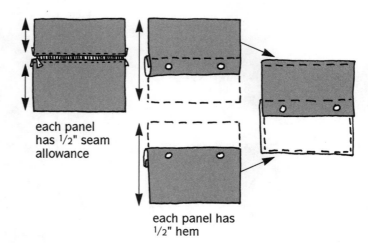

each panel has ½" seam allowance

each panel has ½" hem

✂ If you want to pad an item more than indicated in the project, measure the girth of the padding and adjust the pattern pieces to fit. This may be as simple as changing one pattern piece, or it may mean changing the dimensions of the entire project.

Designing Your Own Projects

If you want to design your own projects, let your knowledge about sewing and geometry, and your ideas as to what you want the end product to be, guide you. Look through catalogs and at similar items in stores — do they have any features you would like to incorporate into your design? Study how they were made at the factory, and whether you can re-create them at home.

Start by drawing what you think you want the product to look like, including possible finished sizes. If it's an item that needs to fit your body or a certain space in your house, measure and design accordingly. Then draw out each pattern piece in small scale, thinking about which edges join each other and must, therefore, be the same length. Can you make one large piece that turns a corner, or would it make more sense to have two or more pattern pieces sewn together at that junction? These are personal decisions, based on your sewing ability and the function of the piece. Remember that a stitch line encourages folding of the fabric, which may or may not be desirable, depending on the design.

Once you think you have all of the pattern pieces sketched, start adding in seam allowances for all seams, hems, casings, edges, and zippers. Decide how wide your hems and casings need to be: Will they need to be wide enough to house a grommet? Do you need three layers to reinforce the grommet, or would you

prefer to use interfacing? How wide is the elastic or drawstring you'll be threading through the casing? Remember to add some ease so the casing can gather smoothly.

Think about how all the pieces will fit together: In what order will you sew the pieces? Would a different kind of pocket look better or be more practical? Do you have a certain trim you've been wanting to use, but it's very wide and means you'll have to add seam allowance to make room for it? Work through this in your mind and make notes — you may find that attaching a piece earlier in the process would have saved you steps later, or that binding an edge would have eliminated bulk that later caused you problems.

Sew a prototype of the project out of muslin or other "throw-away fabric." There will be some rough spots, but when you solve them, you'll have a custom pattern that uses your favorite sewing methods, fulfills a practical use in your life, and is your own creation! Make notes for your pattern, because it may be something you save and make again years from now — and you won't remember all the details.

After you have worked out the kinks using your prototype, get out the good fabrics and start sewing. All the work you put into the design and planning pays off when you can breeze through the cutting and sewing of your own pattern, knowing that it will work.

The projects in chapters 3 through 7 went through the prototype process in my studio, and believe me, I used a lot of "throw-away fabric"! The sizes, shapes, and details of these designs suited my ideas of form and function. It is my hope that as you work through some of these projects, you will become familiar with the techniques, gain an understanding of how and why things were designed the way they were, and start planning how you could improve upon my designs to better suit your needs and your aesthetic sense.

Now, let's run through a few complex projects, and the thought processes required to design them. I raise some questions along the way, that exemplify the questions you should ask yourself when designing your own projects. By deciding how you want to make the projects and by working through these questions, you will increase your understanding of technical design for practical sewing.

Tool Tote

Say you want to design a tote bag with pockets all around the inside and the outside. Think through the various tote patterns based on a "cross shape" (like the Grocery Bag on page 86). You could place pockets on each panel and then stitch the side seams together, but is this the best way? Wouldn't it make the seams bulky?

What if you made the sides from one continuous piece of fabric (that wraps around the circumference of the bag), with the pockets extending the full length, and then add the bottom? Or, could you devise a pattern in which the bottom is a part of the main pattern piece? If you like one of these ideas, decide how large a bag you want, and add seam allowances for the join seams and the top edge.

Now you have to design the pockets. Flat? Pleats? Pouch? The size and shape of the pockets should depend on what tools need to fit inside of them. Do you want the inner pockets to be flat against the inner walls, or billow out to fill the inside of the bag? Measure the full length of the bag walls, and design a continuous row of pockets that will finish the same length.

Remember that once you have stitched on the inner (or outer) pockets, the seams used to sew on the other set will go through all layers. Therefore, have both layers use the same partition lines, or design them so that the partition lines of the second set divide the first set into smaller, planned compartments.

Add seam allowances to the sides and bottom of the pockets and decide if you want the raw edges to be stitched into the seam allowances of the bag, or hemmed under to eliminate bulk in the seam. For a one-piece bag pattern, there is no seam along one edge (where the bottom is formed by a continuous flap extension). How should the pocket be attached along that edge? The choice is yours.

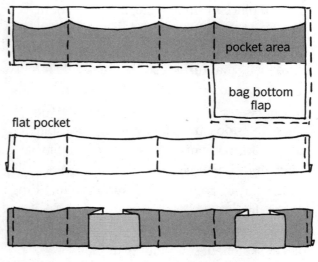

flat pocket

pleated pocket requires much longer pattern piece

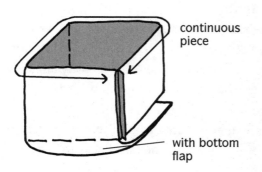

continuous piece

with bottom flap

How will the pocket tops be finished? They could be bound, hemmed, or finished with elastic casings (which will ensure that the tops stay taut). Sketch in the seam allowances or casing lines for the finish you have chosen.

Now address the handles of the bag. How will you attach them? Do you plan to carry a lot of weight? If so, you might consider strap webbing around the bottom. Will this work with the pocket divisions you have chosen? It may be necessary to go back and redesign the pockets where the strap webbing needs to go, to locate the 1-inch webbing between two pockets. Is your bag large enough to allow you to stitch the webbing on through the inside of the bag after the side seams are sewn? If not, is there a way to attach the webbing before sewing the bag together? Decide whether to change the handles or the bag itself.

Next, decide if you should stitch the top bag edge binding on before you add the handles, or end the handles shy of the top edge and attach the seam binding last.

You can begin to see how many issues must be considered. I try to work them out on paper, but it's easy to forget small details. That's why I highly recommend the use of scrap fabrics for the first prototype. There are tons of details to attend to, and if you personalize all of these features, I guarantee that your bag will be unlike anyone else's.

Summertime Bedroll

To make a simple bedroll with a waterproof bottom, zip-closed bag, some padding, and a comfortable, breathable, lining fabric, I might choose pack cloth for the waterproof outer covering, a prequilted batting for the padding, polar fleece for the blanket, and cotton flannel for the lining. Let's start sketching.

If the waterproof bottom extended beyond the sleeping area, you'd be more likely to stay dry, so decide how long and wide you want the sleeping roll to be, and add a border to determine the size of the waterproof piece.

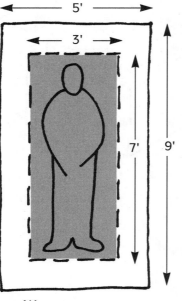

WATERPROOF LINER

The bedroll has to be twice the finished size so that it will fold over you and zip shut. It also has to be large enough to compensate for the volume taken up by whatever padding you choose. Select your padding, and use a tape measure to measure around a piece to see how much fabric you should add to cover it. (This is guesswork!) Will both the top and bottom layers be padded, or will you have padding beneath you, and a simple blanket over you? You may carry a separate pad when you camp, and, therefore, won't need padding at all.

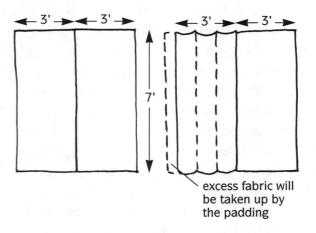

excess fabric will be taken up by the padding

Do you want the zipper to round the corner or just go down one edge? Or would you rather use hook and loop or snaps? Should the top layer extend up all the way (over your head), or should it end 8 to 12 inches lower, like a blanket would? This decision will determine whether the roll is made of one large piece of fabric or two pieces of different sizes that are sewn or bound together.

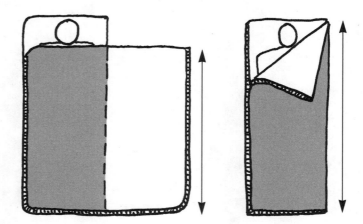

Start sketching the individual pattern pieces, and think about how to attach the fasteners without having all those layers in the seam. You'll need to make pattern pieces for the flannel liner, the polar fleece blanket, and the waterproof outer covering. Some topstitching will be required to hold everything in place, and you will need to devise a way to attach the fasteners only to the layers they actually fasten. You may need to stitch all layers together an inch or two from the seam allowance and then trim all layers back except the ones you will sew to the zipper. There are several other ways to accomplish this task. Experiment with small samples to see what works.

You'll want this entire package to roll up for storage. Will the waterproof flaps fold in, and then the bag fold in half before rolling? Will this be too thick to carry? Will you use ties or separate bungee cords? If you use ties, where will they be located, and how will they be attached? Should they be stitched to the waterproof layer only?

To be sure that any crucial details haven't been forgotten, I'd make a small version (with a 10-inch zipper?), or a full-size muslin version before making one with fabric. This is pretty complex, so be patient!.

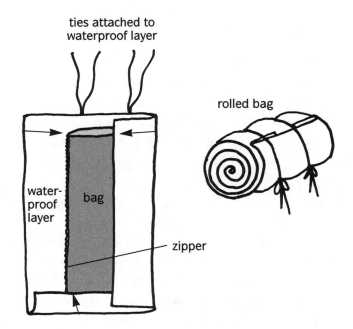

ties attached to waterproof layer

rolled bag

water-proof layer

bag

zipper

Dog Bed

I have made several beds for my pets, and each time, I add to or modify the pattern to fit the animal, the available fabric, the space in the house or whatever factors seem important at the time. My current pet, a Welsh Corgi, is long in the body and short in the legs. He's 40 inches long and about 12 inches high, so he needs a bed shaped like a hot dog bun. The bed I made consists of an oval mattress cover with a zipper around one end. My dog loves to sleep with his head on a pillow, so I built one into his bed, similar to a bolster on a couch. I fastened 2-inch wide hook and loop strips along the top of the bed, placed around the back and side edges, and made a very flexible bolster that curves around the oval. Hook and loop along the bottom of the bolster fastens it to the mattress. Both the mattress and the bolster covers zip open so I can remove the stuffing and wash them.

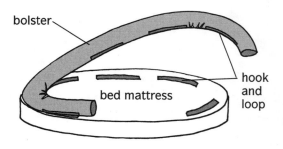

Another option would be to make a foam shape with a built-in bolster, and use spray adhesive to connect the foam forms. Then, design the pattern pieces necessary to cover the shape with one cover. Examine slipcovers and covers on odd-shaped sofa cushions to get ideas. By using welting and side panels cut to the thickness of the foam, you can, relatively easily, cover almost any shape.

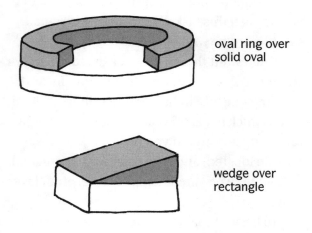

oval ring over solid oval

wedge over rectangle

Measure your pet when sleeping in a stretched-out position. How much space, and what general shape does he or she fill? Do you want to make a simple cushion? If so, use the instructions for the Mattress Pad Cover on page 126. A zip-off cover is a must — it allows you to wash the bed. What will you use for filler? Foam, batting, cedar chips? Do you want to make an inner liner bag to hold the filler when you remove the cover? Will the bed stand by itself, or will it fit inside a box, basket, or other structure?

You can make a padded box for your pet without sewing a stitch — just use a staple gun! Look at pet beds for sale in stores, and customize one to fit your pet.

Saw Blade Holder

My husband has asked me several times for a round saw blade holder, to house his circular saw blades and protect his hands and the blade edges. Round pockets with flaps are required. In addition, the sharp blade edges will cut the fabric if I do not insert something to protect them. After months of thinking about this, I decided on plastic tubing cut in half, running along the inner periphery of the pockets and the flaps.

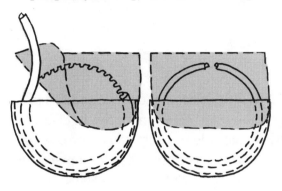

We discussed a hanging rack for the blades, in which the pockets would hang one over the other, like pouches. We also discussed a portable blade holder, set up like a file box that

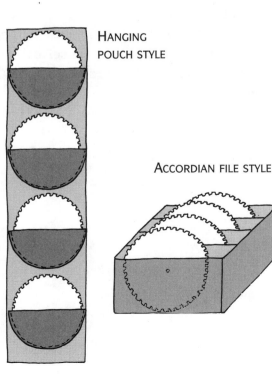

HANGING POUCH STYLE

ACCORDIAN FILE STYLE

he could flip through and pull blades from. This would require a rigid bottom — possibly fabric covered — made of plywood or pressboard.

These "pockets" are similar to a simple portfolio with one large opening, but there are many other considerations. I have not yet designed this item, but I know that the following will have to be considered.

- I need to make different pocket sizes for each blade diameter.
- If I make a file-box style holder, the outer dimension of each pocket should, most likely, be the same as the box, regardless of the blade size.
- Pocket pattern pieces will have to be designed around the bulk of the plastic tubing. Should the tubing be glued under the top flap, or should a continuous piece of tubing extend out from the pocket, which would be manually placed over the exposed blades each time the blade were returned to the pocket?
- Should the pocket flaps be simple, flat flaps, or should they be rounded around the blade to protect against cutting fingers?
- What kind of glue should I use to attach the tubing?
- Do these pocket flaps have to fasten shut, or will gravity hold them down?

I know that the basic shape will be a simple, rounded pocket, but if my husband decides that he wants the pockets connected to each other, instead of separate folios sitting in a file box, this will complicate matters. Do I stitch them to a bottom flap on which they can hinge? Do I hang them from a backing? Should they overlap each other or hang one above the other? Each of these decisions will change the pattern pieces and the order of the sewing steps. Although I haven't yet found the time to design this saw blade holder, it's always in the back of my mind as I sew and shop, and look at similar constructions for ideas.

Accordion File

Think about making a fabric box with file dividers sewn in. How would you do it? At first, the project sounds relatively easy. However, many decisions need to be made regarding putting it all together.

✂ You could make the file with separate fabric pieces for each divider and the finished top and bottom. Then you could turn under and stitch the top and bottom to the side panels of the box to finish.

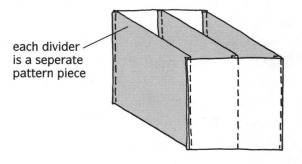

each divider is a seperate pattern piece

✂ You could plan the box sides and pocket divider so that one long length of fabric could accordion back and forth across the side panels to create the front, back, and divider panels. After these dividers are sewn, how will you attach the bottom of the box? Is there a way to stitch the bottom without the seam allowances ending up on the outside of the box? One

solution would be to work in the design element of exposed, bound seam allowances, to create the ties, and make the file more decorative.

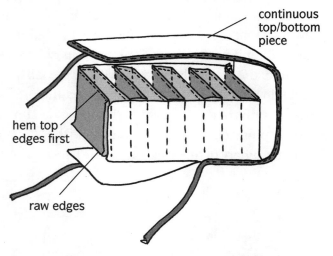

continuous top/bottom piece

hem top edges first

raw edges

This is a project that can be modeled in paper, and then folded and taped in place. A paper visual aide can help you figure out the length of the "accordioned" pattern piece and how it all fits together. I have played around with this one for quite a while and still haven't come up with a design that feels complete, well balanced, and easy to put together. Someday, though, I know I will.

Through these experiences, you can begin to learn how much goes into the design process. Design elements can create technical dilemmas, but learning new techniques helps solve these dilemmas and allows more flexibility in your designs.

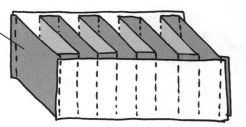

one continuous piece of fabric

Why Design Your Own Patterns?

I'm certain that we learn more from our failures than from our successes. It is the process, the trial and error, that teaches us and helps us grow into more creative people.

There are no limitations to what is possible, because we invent as we go along. I'm sure there are many who know more about technical design than I do. But I'm practical. I like to make useful things, and I learn by doing.

Once we overcome our fear of making mistakes, we allow ourselves the freedom to create. The multidimensional world of sewing, combined with the colors and textures of limitless fabric options, can be the sparks that light our imaginations and put our hidden knowldge and intuition to work.

I hope that the ideas, suggestions, and projects offered in this book have made you more comfortable with the idea of sewing in new ways, of working with shape and seams to elevate sewing to the creative medium it is truly meant to be.

Source List

In addition to fabric, craft, hardware and surplus stores, there are several mail-order companies that sell practical fabrics and findings. Here are some of my favorites.

Airtex — Consumer Products Division
Box 880, 150 Industrial Park Road
Cokato, Minnesota 55321
800-851-8887
Minimum order: 1 case
Filling, form, and foam products

Altanta Thread and Supply Company
695 Red Oak Road
Stockbridge, Georgia 30281
800-847-1001
Minimum order: $20
Sewing supplies, trims, and findings

Buffalo Batt and Felt
Division of Leggett and Platt
3307 Walden Avenue
Depew, New York 14043
716-683-4100, ext. 130
Polyester batting and pillows

Campmor
P.O. Box 700-C
Saddle River, New Jersey 07458-0700
800-226-7667
Findings, webbing, and other practical outdoor items

Clothcrafters
Elkhart Lake, Wisconsin 53020
800-876-2009
100 percent cotton bulk cheesecloth

Clothilde, Inc.
1909 S.W. First Avenue
Fort Lauderdale, Florida 33315-2100
800-772-2891
Sewing tools and notions

Dharma Trading Company
P.O. Box 150916
San Rafael, California 94915
800-542-5227
Fabrics, garment blanks, and decorating supplies

Gohn Brothers
Box 111, 105 South Main
Middlebury, Indiana 46540-0111
219-825-2400
Practical fabrics, findings, and notions

Home-Sew
P.O. Box 4099
Bethlehem, Pennsylvania 18018-0099
800-344-4739
Sewing and craft supplies

Newark Dressmaker Supply
6473 Ruch Road
Lehigh, Pennsylvania 18002-0730
800-736-6783
Fabric, sewing, and craft supplies

Rupert, Gibbon and Spider, Inc.
P.O. Box 425
Healdsburg, California 95448
800-442-0455
Silk and cotton fabrics, and decorating supplies

Sewing Emporium
P.O. Box 5049, 1079 Third Avenue
Chula Vista, California 92010
619-420-3490
Sewing and sewing machine supplies

Steinlauf and Stoller, Inc.
239 West 39th Street
New York, New York 10018
800-637-1637
Fabrics, trims, findings, and machine accessories

Testfabrics, Inc.
P.O. Box 420
Middlesex, New Jersey 08846
908-469-6446
Basic fabrics

Van Dyke's Restorers
P.O. Box 278
Woonsocket, South Dakota 57382
800-558-1234
Upholstery tools, supplies, and basic fabrics

Vaughan Bros., Inc.
P.O. Box 14158
Portland, Oregon 97293
503-228-6485
Industrial and outdoor fabrics and findings

Suggested Reading

Listed here are some books that offer other practical sewing projects. There are many categories that this subject can be divided into, including decorative domestic items, childrens toys and games, or camping and hiking supplies, to name a few. Look in your local library under the headings that interest you most.

If you are interested in learning more about textiles and fibers, there are dozens of textbooks on the subject, available at libraries and many college bookstores. Newer books will offer you the most current technical information. Older textbooks are a great source for learning about natural fiber harvesting and processing, and about the early development of synthetic fibers.

Bennett, Hal Zina. *Sewing for the Outdoors — A Seamster's Guide.* New York: Clarkson N. Potter, 1980.

Chilton Book Company, eds. *The Complete Step-by-Step Guide to Home Sewing.* Radnor, PA: Chilton Book Company, 1990.

Consumer Guide, eds. *The Whole Sewing Catalog.* New York: Simon and Schuster, 1979.

Gheen, W. Lloyd. *Upholstery Techniques Illustrated.* Blue Ridge Summit, PA: Tab Books, 1986.

Honck, Carter, and Myron Miller. *The Big Bag Book.* New York: Charles Scribner's Sons, 1977.

Kinser, Charleen. *Sewing Sculptures.* New York: M. Evans and Company, Inc., 1977.

Perry, Patricia, ed. *The Vogue Sewing Book.* New York: Vogue Patterns, 1970.

Wingate, Isabel B. *Textile Fabrics and Their Selection.* 6th ed. Upper Saddle River, NJ: Prentice-Hall, Inc., 1970.

Wolff, Colette. *The Art of Manipulating Fabric* Radnor, PA: Chilton Book Company, 1996.

Other Storey Titles You Will Enjoy

Decorative Stamping, by Sasha Dorey. A step-by-step guide to a popular method for decorating nearly any surface. 96 pages. Hardcover. ISBN 0-88266-809-9.

Design and Make Fabric Window Shades, by Heather Luke. Detailed instructions and color illustrations accompany more than thirty creative treatments, from simple Roman and roller blinds to glorious cascade and Austrian designs. 80 pages. Hardcover. ISBN 0-88266-895-1.

Design and Make Your Own Curtains and Drapes, by Heather Luke. Written for all abilities, this handbook of more than twenty-five windiow treatment projects includes fully illustrated instructions for layered silk sheers, embroidered linen drapes, heavyweight door curtains, and more. 80 pages. Hardcover. ISBN 0-88266-850-1.

Gifts for Bird Lovers, by Althea Sexton. Step-by-step instructions and illustrations for creating more than fifty projects that will delight birds and bird lovers. 128 pages. Paperback. ISBN 0-88266-981-8.

Gifts for Herb Lovers, by Betty Oppenheimer. Step-by-step instructions and illustrations for creating gifts for the body, gardener, and home. 128 pages. Paperback. ISBN 0-88266-983-4.

Making Your Own Jewelry, by Wendy Haig Milne. Beautiful color illustrations and photos show how to transform beads, semiprecious stones, pearls, crystals, wood, and wire into wearable works of art. 96 pages. Hardcover. ISBN 0-88266-883-8.

Making Your Own Paper, by Marianne Saddington. Step-by-step instructions and color illustrations explain how to use a mold, press and dry, color and texture, prepare a writing surface, and create paper arts and crafts. 96 pages. Paperback. ISBN 0-88266-784-X.

Nature Printing with Herbs, Fruits & Flowers, by Laura Donnelly Bethmann. Step-by-step instructions for applying paint directly to plants and flowers to press images onto stationery, journals, fabrics, walls, furniture, and more. 96 pages. Paperback. ISBN 0-88266-929-X.

These and other Storey titles are available at your bookstore, farm store, garden center, or directly from Storey Books, Schoolhouse Road, Pownal, Vermont 05261, or by calling 800-441-5700. www.storey.com